Social Work with Children

LIBRARY OF SOCIAL WORK

GENERAL EDITOR: NOEL TIMMS
Professor of Social Work Studies
University of Newcastle-upon-Tyne

Social Work with Children

Juliet Berry
Department of Sociological Studies
University of Sheffield

LONDON, HENLEY AND BOSTON

ROUTLEDGE & KEGAN PAUL

First published 1972
by Routledge & Kegan Paul Ltd
39 Store Street
London WC1E 7DD,
Broadway House, Newtown Road
Henley-on-Thames
Oxon. RG9 1EN and
9 Park Street
Boston, Mass. 02108, U.S.A.
Reprinted 1976
Printed in Great Britain by
Redwood Burn Limited
Trowbridge and Esher

ISBN 0 7100 7267 8 (c)
ISBN 0 7100 7268 6 (p)

General editor's introduction

The Library of Social Work is designed to meet the needs of students following courses of training for social work. In recent years the number and kinds of training in Britain have increased in an unprecedented way. The Library will consist of short texts designed to introduce the student to the main features of each topic of enquiry, to the significant theoretical contributions so far made to its understanding, and to some of the outstanding problems. Each volume will suggest ways in which the student might continue his work by further reading.

Juliet Berry has not chosen an easy subject. The knowledge on which social work with children might be based could be seen either as unnecessary (we all know how to look after children) or unreliable (the theories put forward are exclusively psychological and untested). Furthermore, there seems something almost indecently deliberate about analysing in detail our reactions to children and their communication with us. These and other difficulties are successfully mastered in this the first book in this country to be devoted exclusively to the subject of social work with children. It is based on a sensitive appraisal of the status of childhood (chapter 1) and a broad conception of the requirements for good social development (chapter 2). At the same time as a rich variety of sources is used (e.g. lullabies and more formal literature) some of the critical questions are not glossed over (e.g. the elusive and difficult concept of need). Detailed attention is given to the subject of casework with children (chapter 3), but other ways of helping children are not ignored (chapter 6 on behaviour therapy, group work and community work, conjoint family therapy and forms of social action). A particularly successful aspect of this work is the way in which the author holds an effective balance between two sets of opposition—so considering the child that his family context is diminished (particularly chapter 5); emphasising 'the child' at the expense of the special circumstances in which he may find himself (see chapter 4).

As in some other volumes in the Library, we are concerned in this book with the attempt to match a particular group of potential and actual users of social service (children—in other books it is immigrants, the mentally subnormal, families and so on) with the methods social workers have at their command. This book has a place in the Library of Social Work both because children constitute an important, because vulnerable, section of the clientèle of the social services and because in considering the similarities between social work with children and such activity with other groups we are given another opportunity of working out in more detail the nature of a specialisation in social work. Furthermore, if we, as it were, hold the users constant while we review the different methods that might be adopted to help them we can begin to grasp the differential impact of the various approaches contained within social work.

NOEL TIMMS

Contents

CONTENTS

Acknowledgments

Typically, I am beholden to many but directly responsible for what follows. Those who influenced me earlier, through their own attitudes towards social work with children, include Lulie Shaw, Wendy Robinson, Margaret Veitch, Elisabeth and Harry Mapstone, other former colleagues and clients of all ages. For their immediate help, I want especially to thank colleagues in Sheffield: Lily Barker, Pamela Mann and Neil Kay. I am also indebted to Noel Timms; to our applied social studies students who are more helpful than they may realise, and to Mrs Grace Tyack for her careful typing.

J.B.

1

Pleasures and pressures of parenthood

When all is done, human life is ... but like a froward child, that must be played with and humoured a little to keep it quiet until it falls asleep, and then the care is over.

(Sir William Temple, 1628-1699)

Childhood can indeed only be defined as the period in a life during which parents are essential, at first to the child's existence and later to his full mental and physical health.

(Fordham, 1964)

These quotations illustrate some of the ideas presented in this introductory chapter about parent-child interactions, and about attitudes towards the responsibilities of parenthood. The first quotation suggests an uneasy resignation, not uncommon today, that children are demanding creatures who must be pacified before the parents can find peace; the second definition tends to exaggerate its own truth, without specifying any positive qualities necessary for adequate parenthood. In writing of parents, I include substitute parents, and shall sometimes refer to the latter as caretakers: that is, any adults bound up with children through giving them daily care. Unfortunately the social work context of the chapter means that it is preoccupied with the pressures rather than with the pleasures of parenthood, and I have included 'pleasures' in its title only as a reminder that most parents experience far more enjoyment than discomfort in their role. The Newsons' record (1968, chapter 15) of mothers' comments on the most delightful things about their four-year-olds, or Laurie Lee's story of his feelings on first becoming a father (1964), might help towards restoring balance to the picture.

In considering the responsibilities of parenthood, perhaps a preliminary question is:

What are the basic needs of any child?

Imagine four eight-year-old boys waiting on a crowded railway platform.

> David is missing school today because of a knee-injury which is being treated by a large bandage and an hour's train-spotting; his coloured friend Micky is playing truant in order to keep him company. Kevin is being received into the care of the local authority, and clutches the sum of his possessions in a cardboard box. Adam, at his parents' considerable financial expense, is going for the first time to a prep-school, and is accompanied by a handsome trunk packed with new clothes and equipment.

Past, present and potential future experience of these four boys is dissimilar, and their adults may have different expectations of them. But I believe the *basic needs* of all four are virtually identical. (The concept of basic human needs is controversial, being considered unproductive by many sociologists. However, Etzioni (1968) presents a case for the usefulness of the concept as he believes it fruitful to assume that there is a universal set of basic human needs which have attributes of their own not determined by social structure, cultural patterns or socialisation processes.) I shall later distinguish between children in contrasting socio-economic groups and in a variety of special circumstances, but first it may be useful to consider generically the fundamental needs of children of every age, class and colour. In listing these, I am looking for a low-adequate common denominator (analogous to Beveridge's plan for a basic minimum standard of living) and am therefore not specifying in detail such as a bed with clean sheets and blankets, but 'a safe, warm place in which to sleep', which may be a quarter of a sagging mattress or a cradle encrusted with diamonds.

At first sight these basic needs of a child seem very simple. *Physically* he needs a small share of a dwelling-place and neighbourhood, some food and clothes, a safe, warm place in which to sleep, a few toys or material objects and an occasional wash. ('Fresh air' has been omitted, as its supposed benefit has sometimes been used as an excuse for removing a child and his problems to an isolated rural community.) *Emotionally* and *socially* he needs some love —not from just anybody but primarily from, and between, the adults he regards as his own; a vague feeling of being wanted and accepted for himself, to be treated fairly consistently and with sufficient firmness to prevent his hurting himself or others, and to have some sense of security and continuity. *Intellectually* he needs some degree of stimulation from his environment; opportunities for play, achievement, and to discover himself in relation to his extending world. In practice these needs are not divisible: for example, the physical giving and eating of food is also a means of giving and receiving love; play provides opportunity for social as well as for physical and mental development.

Such areas of need tend to be identified more through consensus of opinion than by research findings. Those who once administered the Poor Law would perhaps not have

3

argued heatedly in principle over my list of physical needs, unless by recommending no toys and greater cleanliness. (George, 1970, gives an account of foster-care in the nineteenth century.) Modern educationalists would endorse the list of intellectual needs, and the current swarm of playgroups arose partly through recognition that children who lack stimulus in their own homes benefit through experiencing it sometimes elsewhere, in rather the same way that young deaf children need early auditory stimulus as a basis for language development. The second group, of emotional and social needs, is the least tangible, and its vital importance has been highlighted in recent years. Bowlby's monograph (1951) asserted that the prolonged maternal deprivation of a young child has serious, long-term effects on his personality, and may result in an affectionless character prone to persistent delinquency.

Bowlby's first work on this theme is undeniably important, but caused some theoretical controversy and, though its practical effects in the child care field have been widely acknowledged as extremely beneficial, its occasional glib acceptance by fieldworkers and administrators may, paradoxically, have resulted in some expedient refusals to remove young children from grossly inadequate or hostile mother-figures on the rationalised grounds that separation would do more harm than good. However, the very controversy and confusion led to further valuable research, which will continue, and those who re-examine the complex evidence may agree with Ainsworth (1962, 1965) that maternal deprivation in early childhood has an adverse effect on development both during the deprivation experience and for a longer or shorter time after deprivation is relieved, and that severe deprivation can lead in some cases to grave effects that resist reversal. Ainsworth points out that the term 'maternal deprivation' has been used to cover a range of undesirable mother-child interactions, and she distinguishes between: *insufficiency* of interaction implicit in deprivation; *distortion* in the character of the interaction without respect to its quantity, and the *discontinuity* of relationships brought about through separation.

Wootton (1962) sees the previous research as useful 'chiefly for its incidental exposure of the prevalence of deplorable patterns of institutional upbringing, and of the crass indifference of certain hospitals to childish sensitivities'. Andry's studies (1962) emphasised the importance of paternal roles, and he recommended that, in future child guidance work, not only the mothers but many more fathers should be involved in the whole treatment programme, especially in the case of delinquents. Young children in hospital have been studied, notably by Robertson (1958), who with his wife's help later extended his concern to observing other brief separation experiences in residential and foster-care. His films depict unmistakably the extreme distress of two-year-old Laura separated for eight days from her parents in a hospital ward; the serious effect on seventeen-month-old John of nine days in residential care with a rota of over-worked staff, and the way in which similar situations are greatly eased when a child's mother is allowed to stay with her (Sally, aged twenty months) in hospital, or when brief foster-care (of Kate, aged two and a half years, and Jane, aged seventeen months) is planned carefully to give some warmth and continuity of experience throughout the period of upheaval. (As an alternative to films, Heinicke and Westheimer, 1965, give pictorial accounts of young children in separation experiences.) Robertson describes three phases of *protest*, *despair* and *detachment* commonly observed in young children who feel, with or without objective reason, they have been deserted by their parents.

The first phase of *protest* may last for a few hours or several days, when the young child has a strong conscious need of his mother and expects, from previous experience, that she will respond to his cries. He is grief-stricken to have lost her, confused and frightened by unfamiliar surroundings, and tries to recapture her by every means in his limited power: loud crying, eager looking, rejecting alternative comfort ... *Despair* gradually follows, characterised by a continuing conscious need of his mother combined with increasing hopelessness: he becomes withdrawn and apathetic, 'in a state of deep mourning' when he may cry monotonously and intermittently, and tends to make few demands of the immediate environment. This quieter stage is sometimes wrongly supposed to indicate the child's acceptance of the situation; it is the stage when current caretakers may resist visits from parents as being unsettling and as causing renewed distress rather than bringing to the surface intense grief and anger that were becoming buried alive. The third phase of *denial/detachment* may ensue when the child can no longer tolerate the intensity of his feelings and 'forgets' his mother, thereby freeing himself to take whatever superficial satisfaction he can find elsewhere—which bodes ill for future relationships in spite of his apparent adjustment. If the separation is brief, young children may return home in the more hopeful phase of despair or even of protest and, if special care and understanding is given before, during and after the separation, emotional damage may be minimised. But it takes time for the child to regain confidence in his parents, and meanwhile he may not even recognise his mother when she first reappears, and is likely to show difficult, aggressive, rejecting, anxious, clinging behaviour, which the worried parents may misconstrue as signs of his having been over-indulged elsewhere.

No subsequent research or theoretical arguments (Ainsworth, 1962; Bowlby, 1965) are sufficient as yet seriously to undermine Bowlby's original statement (1951):

What is believed to be essential for mental health is that the infant and young child should experience a warm, intimate and continuous relationship with his mother (or permanent mother substitute) in which both find satisfaction and enjoyment ... It is this complex, rich and rewarding relationship with the mother in the early years, varied in countless ways by relations with the father and with siblings, that child psychiatrists and many others now believe to underlie the development of character and of mental health.

The ideas promoted by Bowlby *et al*. have such far-reaching implications that it is tempting to swallow or to criticise them somewhat blindly when one is faced with situations involving the risk of separation. Though it is agreed now that not all children suffering early maternal deprivation are scarred identically and indelibly, so many factors are involved that it is not easy to predict an individual child's vulnerability. Perhaps Bowlby himself draws the only reasonable conclusion: the separation of a young child from his mother-figure is not to be undertaken without weighty reasons and then only provided there is a suitable and stable substitute available. In practical terms, parents and workers should do all in their power to avoid such separation but, if it is inevitable, much can be done before, during and after the experience to ameliorate its potentially damaging effects.

Even this working compromise leaves us with some very difficult decisions, not least in knowing the point at which removal of a child from an unsatisfactory home environment is likely to be less harmful than leaving him where he is. And do the risks inherent in separation take priority over all other considerations? For example: a little girl aged six is now happily settled in a long-term foster-home, but she is still unable to talk, and has not responded to treatment available locally—is it in her interests to go for at least a year to an excellent boarding-school which specialises in treating speech disorders? Or again, a boy aged three has been brought up since birth by his healthy grandparents because of his mother's temporary mental illness and subsequent disappearance: now she has re-appeared and is determined to make a good home for him a hundred miles away—where does he belong? Some of the considerations surrounding these dilemmas will be explored in later chapters. Meanwhile the question of children's needs may be summed up by Pringle (1969, pp. 5-8) who interprets the concept of 'child care' not as an emergency rescue operation but, in its widest sense, as relevant to all children whether or not they live with their own families, whether they are 'normal' or handicapped, and as implying that *all children need care, and special care at certain times in their lives.*

The list of basic needs of all children does not sound too exacting or difficult to satisfy in ordinary circumstances. But the task can be almost impossible for parents who were themselves chronically unsatisfied in childhood, and whose own current needs exert such pressure that they cannot easily recognise or meet the demands of their children. The natural demands of young children are long-term and ever-present, and should not be underestimated, especially when other pressures are heavy—pressures such as poor health, low income, inadequate housing and unsupportive marital relationships. It seems that a contented child is usually a 'good' child, and that unhappy children with unmet needs are more difficult to look after—either by their parents or by anyone else. (Trasler, 1960, concluded that young children tend to interpret separation from their parents as the withdrawal of affection, and that this causes difficulty in subsequent adjustment to caretakers. Le Masters, 1965, and Dyer, 1965, both studied parents' sense of crisis arising from the birth of their first child.) Social workers may sometimes be helpful in recognising sympathetically with parents that children can be maddening in their incessant demands, and that it is both natural and painful to feel ambivalent towards them.

An important additional pressure is the complex expectations adults have of themselves in their parental role, often causing chagrined shame if their child 'shows them up', and the expectations of society for its children in the mass.

Attitudes of society towards its children

At first sight again, society's attitude towards children appears to be a positive one of whole-hearted concern. It is hardly possible to generalise objectively in three paragraphs about sections of society in this country, but a social worker cannot help noticing certain broad trends and tendencies which imply ambivalence towards dependent groups and towards their strivings for independence. Children on the whole are welcomed as a blessing, and happy is he who has his quiverful, within reason. Society invests a good deal—financial and emotional—in its children, the emotional becoming more important as children are visualised less as potential wage-earners, with more people claiming a right to 'happiness'. But as one ages, it is not easy to watch growing children make a take-over bid for the future. Victorian children were supposed to be seen and not heard, but modern adolescents can be offensive to older people even in their physical appearance. Musgrove (1964) discusses varying attitudes towards young people in the last two hundred years, and suggests that the adolescent was invented, by Rousseau, at the same time as the steam engine, and that society has subsequently had the problem of how to accommodate him in the social structure. Though Musgrove quotes studies suggesting that adolescents, in their moral values and in their personality traits, differ little from mature adults, his own research showed considerable agreement amongst adults that adolescents should inhabit a segregated and virtually autonomous, non-adult social sphere rather than be welcomed as legitimate participants in adult life. In a further survey, Musgrove found that adolescents tend to be more kindly disposed towards adults than are the latter towards youth.

There is something hopeful about the concept of children, a feeling that we shall live on in them and that they may salvage our disappointments. In this sense, we almost prefer to keep children in a state of Wordsworthian innocence, and tend to gloss over their questions about birth, death and suffering. A photograph on the dustcover of *The Evacuees* (ed. Johnson, 1968) shows how adults try to keep up brightly smiling appearances when involved with children in painful situations. As well as gaining enormous vicarious enjoyment through sharing the untarnished pleasures of childhood, adults tend to envy the apparently carefree early years, and simultaneously there is a fear that the uninhibited nature of children will somehow get beyond control and upset our established scene. Although a baby is the epitome of puny helplessness, the sheer violence of its importunate cries can be alarming. Nowadays there is tension between anxiety not to 'repress' a child and fear lest he get out of hand from earliest babyhood. Society makes sacrifices for the future generation, and expects a tangible expression of grateful behaviour in return. Deprived and otherwise handicapped children are often expected to be particularly grateful for public favours received, but in practice they rarely are at the time, and there is no reason why they should be.

We were all children once (and still frequently are) and therefore presume to have real knowledge of childhood. 'Experts' in the field of child care tend either to be pooh-poohed or to be regarded as magicians. Some sections of the general public, on the basis of their own experience, are ready with advice especially for new parents, who can be confused by conflicting suggestions and therefore lack confidence in their own natural ability. J. Klein (1965) collected evidence on patterns of child-rearing practices in diverse socio-economic groups, and discusses some of the strains of moving from traditional patterns into self-conscious uncertainty through social mobility and even by reading books on child-rearing, which may be 'a very frightening form of culture-contact'. Adopters and their children (similarly foster-parents) are not infrequently pained by insensitive comments on their circumstances. People are easily sentimental over the misfortunes of children of any class, creed or colour, but less willing to provide public support for a proportion of 'unrespectable parents' upon whom these children depend. However, attitudes do change gradually. Changes in law begin to imply that children are regarded less as possessions. Delinquent children, who would have been hanged for stealing less than two hundred years ago, nowadays receive somewhat more therapeutic treatment. Perhaps society's attitude to children is partially expressed in the toys it provides for them : the prim, elaborately-dressed dolls of the Victorians; the sexless, celluloid baby dolls in the earlier part of this century, giving way now to sophisticated figures which leave smaller scope for the imagination. (Coveney, 1967, reviews the portrayal of children in literature; Pinchbeck and Hewitt, 1969, examine changing social attitudes towards children in England since Tudor times.)

Ambivalence of parents towards their children

Parents are part of society and share some of its attitudes, but are far more deeply involved and vulnerable in relation to their own children. Perlman (1968) says that parenthood requires a basic, consistent, continuous willingness to give or lend oneself to the nurture and protection of another ... 'And more: because the child is a growing person in a sequence of evolving life-stages under changing circumstances, the parental role has perforce to change and develop alongside.' The complex interaction between mothers and children is well illustrated in the Newsons' accounts (1963, 1968) of a research project which aims to discover what 700 Nottingham mothers feel about their children, and how they react in practice to all the situations which arise daily in bringing up a family. These mothers, from various social classes, talk with vivid spontaneity of their role in caring for babies, and later of almost the same sample of children as four-year-olds, and it will be fascinating to continue hearing of this large group.

Rather than range widely over the numerous daily situations which may arouse parental ambivalence, I would like to look at a particular event in the child's bed-time, through considering some of the feelings and attitudes expressed in lullabies. (This is in keeping with the idea of both Bettelheim (1950) and Dockar Drysdale (1968) that it is valuable in residential life to focus on a particular situation for study.) Initially I turned to the *Oxford Nursery Rhyme Book*, assembled by the Opies, expecting to find an example of a warm parent-child relationship, as children are often said to be at their most lovable when nearly asleep. The sixteen lullabies in one section of their book are presumably a random selection, chosen largely to illustrate 'the heritage of our oral tradition', which may be expected to give some indication of ordinary human sentiments over many generations. In choosing to quote seven lullabies from the total number of sixteen, I am not omitting those which show much greater warmth of affection: however, it may be agreed that the accompaniment of rocking/nursing/tone of voice could express unrecorded love, leaving the actual words free to express other emotions. (This in turn raises the question of how much children do hear, even when they do not seem to be listening.)

1. *Hushie ba, burdie beeton,*
   Your Mammie's gone to
   Seaton
   For to buy a lammie's
   skin

1. This lullaby, like most of those omitted, has comparatively few emotional undertones, and implies hopefully that, even if the mother

*To wrap your bonnie
boukie in.*

leaves her baby, the short separation will be in the child's best interests.

2. *I'll buy you a tartan
bonnet
And feathers to put on it,
With a hush-a-bye and
a lullaby,
Because you are so like
your Daddy.*

2. This too seems pleasant enough, but is there a slight suggestion of conditional love? Will the bonnet be removed if he strives for individuality in toddlerhood —not to mention adolescence?

3. *Bye, bye, baby bunting,
Your Daddy's gone
a-hunting,
Your Mummy's gone
the other way,
To beg a jug of sour whey
For little baby bunting.*

3. A song for granny/foster-mother/baby-sitter to sing. She may be describing a home where the parents are secure in their complementary roles, or is there a hint of marital disharmony? There is certainly a note of poverty (still a major factor even in our modern Welfare State) though the sour whey in its day would be palatable and nourishing.

4. *Hush little baby, don't
say a word,
Papa's going to buy you
a mocking bird.*

*If the mocking bird
won't sing,
Papa's going to buy you
a golden ring.*

*If the golden ring
turns to brass,
Papa's going to buy you
a looking-glass.*

4. Is this an enjoyable flight of fantasy, or perhaps two parents trying to pacify their 'spoilt' child? It sounds as though they will go to endless trouble to *buy* the child 'everything she wants', but in fact there is little satisfaction in these broken-reed-type presents, and even the climax of a second billy-goat has limited charms. So the first impression, of a whin-

If the looking-glass
           gets broke,
Papa's going to buy you
           a billy-goat.

If that billy-goat runs
           away
Papa's going to buy you
           another today.

ing child being over-indulged, broadens to a picture of parents who fear their child's emotional demands as excessive. ('Don't say a word.') Through gaining little emotional satisfaction, the child increases her demands, and appears 'spoilt'.

5. Hush-a-baa, baby,
   Dinna mak' a din
   An' ye'll get a cakie
   When the baker comes
           in.

5. This mother uses her own dialect instead of the scientific jargon of behaviour therapists. The latter would consider her method inappropriate in babyhood. Of course she will have to train her child in some ways later on, but one hopes she will not make a damaging issue out of emotionally-laden situations such as toilet-training.

6. Baby, baby, naughty
           baby,
   Hush, you squalling thing
           I say.
   Peace this moment, peace,
           or maybe
   Bonaparte will pass this
           way.

Baby, baby, if he hears
           you,
As he gallops past the
           house,
Limb from limb at once
           he'll tear you,

6. The lullaby of a battering parent, or a potential one. Even if it were sung 'in fun', the child would be sleepless with excited laughter. The singing of these words may prevent an actual attack, as the wish to beat is projected on to a bogey-man. The words fit with recent understanding of battering parents, who may be distressed beyond endurance by the baby's crying, and perceive it as a critical de-

*Just as pussy tears a
        mouse.*

*And he'll beat you, beat
        you, beat you,
And he'll beat you all to
        pap,
And he'll eat you, eat
        you, eat you,
Every morsel, snap, snap,
        snap.*

(Three out of four verses.)

mand. It is typical too that
the child's identity is mis-
perceived—this one is a
'thing'.

7. *Hush-a-bye, baby,
        The beggar shan't have
                'ee
No more shall the mag-
                gotty-pie,
The rooks nor the ravens
Shan't carry 'ee to
                heaven,
So hush-a-bye, baby, bye-
                bye.*

(maggotty-pie=magpie)

7. The lullaby of an 'over-
protective' mother, and a
good example of reassur-
ance at its most unhelpful!
It conveys a subtle threat
in that she need not have
mentioned the possibility of
these misadventures. It is a
message of hostility dis-
guised as protective con-
cern, and her child will
easily become over-anxious.
The previous 'lullaby' was
only the other side of the
same coin.

Clearly it was naïve to have supposed that lullabies would
portray uncomplicated parental affection: the mother has
been coping with her child all day, so she is likely to feel
exasperated if her child struggles against sleep. Perhaps
contented babies do not need to be sung to sleep; neither
do fretful children evoke soothing words. But bed-time is
not typically more fraught than is meal-time, bath-time
or potty-time, so it seems reasonable to look at what
mothers may be feeling then. The seven lullabies provide
clues about a range of problems which may arise in the

parent-child relationship. Even if modern mothers do not use traditional lullabies, it seems that many of them *review* their child's day when putting him to bed, and may feel a rush of affection for the toddler who is suddenly 'good', or petulant, because he is tired out, mixed with regret for several unnecessary battles with him.

Much of the above was about mothers: however, it is not only they who are capable of carrying out 'mothering activities', but also fathers, teachers, childless adults, residential staff of all kinds, older siblings and others. It would be unfortunate if the main impression gained from this first chapter were merely that parent-figures have clay feet. Indeed it is remarkable that most parents are *'good enough'*, to use D. Winnicott's useful description (1957/64) and that most children grow up in reasonably happy circumstances. We are not in a position to criticise any of the Opie lullaby-singers, even those who seem extreme. In fact destructive criticism is the response most likely to harden their negative attitudes by confirming their worst fears. It is likely, in psycho-social terms, that each parent is simply repeating (or reacting against) the emotional content of the 'song' sung to him or her in distant childhood, and passing on those catch-tunes characteristic of the neighbourhood group/social class. Heinicke and Westheimer (1965, p. 64) find:

> The mothers most able to respond to the child's communications are those whose own personal needs do not obtrude and who have only a minimum of preconceived ideas. Thus they are able to consider the child as an individual and are interested in his expression of individuality. They want to listen and to understand and enjoy the flow of communication between him and them.

A family caseworker, hoping to improve the emotional climate of children at risk, cannot completely counteract damage simply by doing the equivalent of singing a friendly tune regularly to a child on its own; nor is it effective to forbid parent-figures to express their negative feelings directly to children, and to follow this with advice on better child care. In subsequent chapters I hope to convey some constructive methods of social work with, and for, children. Chapters 4 and 6 contain condensed reference sections; chapters 2, 3 and 5 are relatively complete in themselves.

2

Helping children in their social development

... the park was full of terrors and treasures ... that small, interior world widened as I learned its names and its boundaries, as I discovered new refuges and ambushes in its miniature woods and jungles ... In that small, iron-railed universe of rockery, gravel path, bowling green, bandstand ... where an ancient keeper was the tyrannous and whiskered snake in the grass one must keep off, I endured, with pleasure, the first agonies of unrequited love, the first slow boiling in the belly of a bad poem ...

(Reminiscences of Dylan Thomas)

When we first met James at 12 years old ... almost any approach from our other children sent him screaming through our house and grounds trying to hide ... He found some security by drawing our woods into his magic world. He drew maps of them in which he created paths and havens, and named almost every tree. He would sit up a tree for hours, contemplating his kingdom. Then he began to name trees after our adults here, and he took one or two staff members down to show them 'his woods'. In this way he began to adjust to aspects of our community by incorporating them into the sphere where he felt safe; and so he could soon be helped to face a little reality elsewhere.

(The staff of Shotton Hall: *Play in Child Care*)

In this chapter I shall look briefly at the main requirements for healthy social development, dwelling particularly on the value of play. The amount of space given to the various facets does not reflect on their relative importance. Little is said under the heading of 'relationships' for instance, partly because their prime importance is implicit throughout. There is also insufficient space to distinguish in detail between children at different ages and stages. For such detail, one might read Isaacs' classic work (1933); Fraiberg's account (1959) of the early 'magic' years or Muller's divisions of the developmental tasks of childhood (1969); and Erikson's 'Eight ages of man' (1950, chapter 7) summarises childhood within the context of a lifetime.

There are different viewpoints about the goals and the process of socialisation: some people see it as the way in which a child learns to interact as a social being; others regard it as the process of taming him to conform to social and cultural norms. Thus, while parent and worker discuss the possibility of a child joining a playgroup, each of them may have rather different, unexpressed expectations of its value. Danziger (1970) presents a far less simplified summary of various conceptions of socialisation. He is useful also in visualising it as something wider than 'the convenient fiction of the parent-child dyad', where the parent is the active and the child the passive partner. In addition to pointing out the need for treating the socialisation process 'in terms of its embeddedness in the system of family relationships,' he stresses that 'the child is socialised by all the social structures in which he participates'. This chapter, about helping children in their social development, embarks with the proviso that

Potentiality for development lies within the child

This is a comforting idea for over-conscientious parents and workers who may, especially when newly plunged into their role, feel personal responsibility for keeping a child or a client alive. For example, a healthy baby was placed for adoption with a woman who sat by its cot throughout the first night to ensure that breathing continued. D. Winnicott (1957/64, pp. 27-8) has spoken of the unnecessary anxiety of some mothers who seem constantly to be urging their babies into maintaining existence, and he states that the child is 'a going concern'. (Similarly most families possess a tendency to remain intact, and casework situations seem to contain their own energy for movement.) Children show great resilience even in the face of unpromising circumstances. Given a healthy baby who is genetically sound and placed in an environment which has the basic essentials for growth, it would in fact, barring accidents, be difficult to prevent development.

If this raises the question of whether heredity is more or less important than environment, the short answer is that both play their part, but social workers naturally tend to have more faith in environmental influences, if only because otherwise they would feel they had an impossibly uphill task. Halsey (1958) studied a caste system and a class system in order to consider the relation between genetics, social structure and intelligence; his research led to the conclusion that the observed differences between social classes in measured intelligence are more likely to be explained by environmental than by genetic factors. Pringle (1969), having stressed the need to minimise ill-effects of adverse genetic or environmental conditions of children at risk, gives evidence that children from socially and culturally underprivileged homes are adversely affected from an early age and cumulatively thereafter, and goes on to recommend 'positive discrimination' if equal educational opportunity is to be more than an attractive slogan.

Growth is an irresistible process, inescapably linked with conflict. If kindly adults can neither cause nor prevent the development of an existing child, it is also true that they cannot ever succeed in smoothing the child's path completely. Within these extremes, adults do have tremendous power either to help or to hinder a child's development. For example, parents may suffer sympathetically when their baby has teething trouble: they cannot prevent teething, nor can they exorcise the pain, but they can make it bearable by tolerating the baby's fretfulness and by comforting him in his distress. Stevenson (1965) describes three inter-connected conflicts going on in the 'ordinary young child', each a part of growing up: the struggles between self-centred love and other-love; between dependence and independence; and between the worlds of fantasy and reality. We can now begin to consider how adults may help children to cope positively with the conflicts inherent in development.

Relationships

Understanding something of psycho-social development leads one to suppose that the saying 'love your neighbour as yourself' is not a pious exhortation so much as a plain statement about the inevitable way in which human beings do interact. Loving oneself in this sense does not imply lasting narcissism: it results from having been loved and in turn it enables one to love others. Early childhood is the appropriate starting-point, although it is not impossible for love to begin later on: perhaps initially within a professional relationship because of the strains involved, and moving from there towards personal relationships. C. Winnicott (1964, p. 11) affirms that the professional *includes* the best of the personal. Parent-figures who are in some way not emotionally 'good enough' may be helped to accept their children through experiencing acceptance themselves. Love and acceptance are hard to define, but they are not sentimental, nor are they evasive of hard reality. C. Winnicott (p. 29) sees acceptance as involving the worker's effort to know a person as an individual of unique value, and as trying 'to reach behind the delinquent act and the deceitful language to the suffering in the human being which causes the symptoms which we see. Acceptance in this sense is in itself a basic therapeutic experience.' She goes on to suggest that such an attitude of acceptance implies acceptance of oneself as another human being and is the hallmark of the professional worker in any therapeutic setting, whether it be a casework agency, a psychiatric clinic or a residential unit.

A 'good relationship' between worker and client (of any age) does not mean superficial pleasantness from both parties, but that the client feels safe enough to express honest feeling. Most people fear that their hostility will either damage the other person or cause him to retaliate, and the *experience* of finding this not to be true of the worker enables clients to feel more comfortable within themselves and in their other relationships. This is particularly relevant to social work for children, as it seems that (apart from their experiencing separation, which may also imply aggression and rejection) parental hostility is most damaging to a child's emotional development (Woodmansey, 1966, 1969, 1971). The question of the development of conscience arises again indirectly in chapters 5 and 6, and it may suffice here to suggest that a healthy conscience is based on affectionate respect rather than on fear of consequences.

Consistency and discipline

'We've tried everything' ... 'We treat them all alike' ...

22

'*We've given the child everything he wants*'. These three remarks are frequently heard when parents ask for help with a difficult child. The first suggests inconsistent handling, with swings between strict control and weak indulgence. It is tempting for social workers to echo the phrase when frustrated in their efforts for 'troubled children' under the Children & Young Persons Act 1969. With choice of treatment left more open to the worker's discretion, there is a danger (when the child/family appears persistently unco-operative) of using threats and running quickly through the gamut of provisions, starting with voluntary supervision but not giving it time to be effective. The second remark overlooks the fact that siblings are not 'all alike', but vary considerably in age, stage, and personality—and therefore in their individual needs, though they attach great weight to their own primitive concept of fairness. Burn (1956), in describing Mr Lyward's work with intelligent, disturbed adolescent boys, writes of his method of occasionally treating a boy with 'deliberate unfairness', in preparation for ordinary life and almost as a mark of favour. This could well be a maturing influence at Finchden Manor, but younger children in care surely have enough 'accidental unfairness' to assimilate. The third remark links back to the fourth lullaby, and suggests that the parents have tried to compensate in irrelevant, extravagant material ways for their difficulty in meeting the child's emotional needs.

Other common remarks are: '*You can't win*', and '*You mustn't let them get away with it*'. A distressed foster-mother once said resentfully to me, 'Of course you are always on the foster-child's side'. It is unfortunate there should be such widespread feeling that, in bringing up children, there are sides to be taken and battles to be won. Fraiberg (1959) conveys the young child's sense of omnipotence through his use of 'magical thinking'; his belief that his actions and his thoughts can bring about events. But, as she says, a magic world is a potentially unstable world, and I would add that presumably such feelings of powerfulness are only the reverse side of the coin of feelings of helplessness. Children under pressure can appear disproportionately powerful partly because their very fear and resentment paralyses them into an attitude of stubborn defiance, and because some of their symptoms (such as toilet-refusal, food- and school-refusal) seem almost impossible for adults to overcome by force. When engaged in battle, adults may become ruthless, forgetting their own superior strength, and win only at the cost of inflicting wounds—the physical being more amenable to treatment than the emotional. The Newsons' research (1968, chapter 13) shows that three-quarters of the Nottingham sample of mothers smack their four-year-olds on average at least once a week, many of them much more often, which 'adds up to a very large number of aggressive acts'.

> 67% use smacking to enforce obedience, 38% in return for telling lies, 58% smack in response to the child attempting to smack the mother (this seems a particularly threatening situation to the mother) and 33% smack for temper-tantrums. Half feel they smack only when angry, 21% only when calm, 25% might be either; 83% believe in smacking and 17% disapprove 'in principle'.

Where force is seen as a legitimate method of exerting control, it seems hardly surprising that we meet parents who become physically afraid of their children when the latter are old enough to hit back with equal strength. What comes over even more strikingly, in the Nottingham study and general experience, is the sheer ingenuity and calculated pitting of wits which many adults consider necessary in the process of compelling children to conform. A young step-father, whose wife was a hard hitter, said virtuously, 'I don't believe in hitting Kim (aged three)

—*the best way to hurt her* is to stop her sweets, or better still, buy a lot of sweets and eat them in front of her'. (One's immediate reaction of distaste is modified to acceptance through realising his own deprivation.)

Probably we believe that the essence of 'good discipline' lies in giving freedom within reasonable limits, and that any necessary 'correction' for a child is only constructive within the context of a meaningful and friendly relationship. But have we as social workers perhaps muddled some parents into guilty uncertainty about their own natural ways of handling children, so that there is a risk of their resorting to alternative harmful methods such as banishing the child to bed, prolonged nagging, silent recrimination, stopping all pocket money? One dare not suggest to Kim's step-father, even supposing his wife were less aggressive, that a friendly spank might be preferable to his professed tactics, because he might take this as permission to assault the child. There is a similar dilemma in residential work—obviously children must be protected by official rules, but does it seem more degrading, cold and calculating if a house-parent has to consult the punishment regulations instead of reacting spontaneously? Possibly the only immediate practical answer to these questions is that workers should when appropriate discuss with parent-figures their ideas about discipline, in an uncritical atmosphere which allows real expression of feelings. (Chapter 5 explores ways of helping punitive adults, and shows the futility of attempts to argue them into friendlier attitudes: a conflict between caretaker and child may be eased when the worker accepts the caretaker's own pressure of feeling in relation to the child.) It is useless for the worker to throw out glib, idealistic statements without giving the caretaker a chance to respond.

This is especially true for prospective foster-parents and house-parents, who are likely to meet particularly testing behaviour, and who may have unexpectedly violent feelings about a specific item such as 'telling lies'. It seems important sometimes to define terms: the worker may be visualising a gentle tap when smacking is mentioned, while the caretaker construes a passive attitude as meaning that hard hitting is permissible. Where there is a problem in handling the child, it is useful to try to involve both parent-figures in discussion. If one parent (typically the working father) appears to be opting out of the situation, the other may be overwhelmed' by the lonely responsibility of the task and is therefore tempted to distort the child's view of the evasive parent, perhaps by manipulating him into an idealised model or into a threatening authority-figure. (Ancona's research in Norway and Italy, 1970, studied the effects on mothers and children of absent fathers.) Social workers too are frequently used by harassed parents as a frightening external disciplinarian and, rather than fall into this impossible role, the worker has to support the parents in helping them to find positive ways of coping.

A worker is not able to give realistic guidance to parents, nor is he in a position to attempt to modify their expectations of their children, unless he is appropriately aware of cultural patterns of child-rearing. J. Klein's work (1965) shows the importance of practical awareness of English culture patterns. To give contrasting examples: the parents in a submerged, deprived group such as Branch Street, tended first to indulge a very young child (largely through needing to indulge their own affectionate impulses) and subsequently to neglect him. And 'the socialisation of the upper-middle-class child is likely to be guided by considerations of what is good for him, often defined ... in terms of a special routine, regularity, self-control and psychological independence'. Kohn's findings (1959) show that working-class parents tend to punish the external consequences of the child's actions, while middle-class parents are more prone to punish the intention behind the action. This begins to link with Danziger's suggestion that the essential difference between socialisation in different social strata lies not entirely in the area of discipline but also in patterns of communication between parents and children. (In relation to the latter, Bernstein's work, 1967, 1970, is mentioned again below and in chapter 3.)

As for consistency: it seems valuable in setting a reliable pattern, but rigid training of the child is at best of short-term benefit to the adult only. Presumably children need to learn that consistency itself is flexible, and that trustworthy grown-ups, being human, give surprises.

A sense of identity

Perhaps if one has a reasonably clear sense of identity, it is hard to imagine what it feels like to be uncertain—possibly something akin to the sensation of being a foreigner which most people feel in taking on a new role, even though this is comparatively superficial. The gradual acquiring of a sense of 'I am myself and no other' (Timms, 1962) is concentrated in pre-school years and again in adolescence. It is bound up with the pattern of a person's past experience, his confidence in having a significant place in the present, and some faith in relation to future expectations. These three facets become welded into a stability which cannot easily be shattered.

The sense of rooted continuity is accompanied by an intricate system of subsidiary roots, in which tiny details accumulate alongside the broader outlines of culture, tradition and education. My tutor once asked me whether I could remember first having awareness of being a separate person. I immediately recalled a previously forgotten incident of my twin-brother and myself, aged perhaps two or three, being on our mother's knee and discovering we could see little images of ourselves in her eyes. We carried the experiment further, and the vaguely significant thing to me at the time was that we each saw just our separate

self in another person's eyes. I have used a personal example here partly because it is in these imperceptible small
happenings, often without words, that the sense accrues
within a family setting. Also the example illustrates the
idea that one does perceive oneself 'through the eyes of
other people' in close relationships, and therefore it matters
whether or not their regard and their responses are kindly.

If much stability lies in having a sufficiently presentable
picture of oneself not to have to redesign it drastically for
internal or external publication, it follows that children
in disrupted, incomplete families and children in care with
dislocated life histories need special opportunities for sorting and assembling their impressions into some kind of
whole. This suggestion is pursued in chapter 4. Meanwhile
the achieving of sexual identity is relevant here, with a
succinct quotation from Timms (1962, p. 47): 'Both
[parents] are involved in the process whereby the child
begins to share love without having to demand constantly
the presence or exclusive attention of one parent. In
sharing the love of father and mother the child begins to
experience the difference between them and to establish
his own sexual identity with the appropriate parent.'

Dependence/independence

Children struggle between wanting to be looked after and
wanting to manage alone, especially during toddlerhood
(Stevenson, 1965) and adolescence (Laycock, 1970). These
concentrated struggles seem to be connected with spurts
in physical development, the considerable effort and frustration involved in mastering new skills, the widening field
of social relationships, the upheavals caused while learning
to cope with strong feelings and drives, and with the
uncertainty inherent in acquiring a sense of identity. There
would be less mess and less progress if infants were not
determined to feed themselves and if teenagers were con-

tent to learn from the experience of their elders. The acute ambivalence of these ugly-duckling stages obviously taxes the patience and understanding of parent-figures, who are simultaneously trying to find a balance between protecting young people from harm and encouraging their development. Some adults feel that adolescents show little dependence nowadays, but there are signs of it in the interludes of listlessness, erratic eating and sleeping habits, vagueness about changing underclothes, 'using the home as an hotel' : the things which provoke parents into saying, 'I don't know why you're wanting a flat of your own when you've no idea how to look after yourself'. Similarly, some of the irritating habits of small children—their egocentric interruption of adult conversation, tactless curiosity, showing off in front of visitors, their social gaffes—can be seen, paradoxically, as attempts to come to terms with the niceties of civilisation. Adolescence gives a second, more appropriate opportunity to observe contradictions in so-called civilisation and to sort out personal priorities.

In their philosophical moments, parents know that awkward phases will pass. However, there is often an irrational fear that a previously amenable child has suddenly changed and become a permanent stranger. (Although many children steal mildly, some parents view this as the first step in a criminal career, and are in danger of fixing a static label on their child's behaviour, thereby reinforcing it. Malewska and Muszyński (1970) studied children's attitudes to theft; found that 70 per cent of their large sample of young Polish adolescents confessed to taking other people's property, and concluded that two factors affect the child's attitude to honesty : the family's standard of living and 'the extent and way the parents satisfy the child's needs'. However, their paper does not imply merely that children steal whatever is not freely given.) Anxiety over 'normal' development shows itself in trivial ways :

for instance, in the comment, 'Mind your face doesn't get stuck like that', when the child is practising grimaces.

The play situation in childhood (and the formation of peer groups in adolescence) seems to provide a comparatively neutral area in which independence may grow. The remainder of this chapter is about

Play and communication

In our culture, play is often defined as opposite to work. To the working adult, play is *recreation*, but the child's play helps towards the *creation* of himself in relation to his world. Erikson (1950, p. 204) suggests that play pretends at ego-mastery and practises it 'in an intermediate reality between phantasy and actuality'. D. Winnicott (1957/64, p. 146) says: 'Play, like dreams, serves the function of self revelation and of communication at a deep level.' These two descriptions reflect part of the difference between 'ordinary play' and play-therapy.

Toys

Most adults, even if they do not actively appreciate the significance of play, do at least see its attraction and tolerate it as a pastime. In poverty-stricken homes there may be only a few broken toys and the children seem to mess about aimlessly. At the other extreme, 'rich' children may be inundated by expensive, complex toys and are bewildered in knowing what to choose. Bernstein and Young (1967) studied social class differences in conceptions of the uses of toys: they concluded that, for the working-class child, a whole order of potential learning may not be available. Also, in so far as the middle-class mother's concept of the use of toys is in harmony with that of the infant-school, then the middle-class child experiences continuity between home and school, and is more likely to benefit on beginning school. Paul Abbatt, a toy-maker of renown, said (1967):

> Toys help children to solve for themselves the problems of growth. They are more tangible than words, more under the control of children, a natural means of expression while the vocabulary is small. We have to provide children with a vocabulary in toys—simple, usable and useful. Such toys will save many of our own words of reproach and annoyance, because the child ... will be in balance, and from his satisfaction in play will come our satisfaction in him.

(Abbatt's view of toys as words indicates some link between Bernstein's two pieces of research in 1967 and 1970.)

It seems that the child's toys act as a passport in widening experience, or as interpreters while children learn the language of living. Freud gave an example (quoted by Erikson, 1950, p. 208) of a boy aged eighteen months repeatedly throwing a cotton reel and pulling it back on a piece of string, as though to reassure himself with a representation of the goings and comings of his mother. Young children in prams often throw out their toys untiringly and may be seeking a relationship with, or testing the patience of, those who replace the toys within reach. The way in which slightly older children give a toy to a visitor, withdraw temporarily and then return to reclaim it, is another method of meeting people and perhaps a gauging of their own acceptability and independence. It may be necessary and inevitable to break playthings sometimes (particularly so with disturbed children) and there is even a certain fellow-feeling with a broken toy, but children probably feel comforted to have their toys mended for them. It is one thing, however, to enjoy the autonomy of breaking one's own toys and quite another to be given someone else's cast-offs—social work agencies which act as a clearing-house for quantities of old toys at Christmas-time need to consider how these reflect on the personal worth of the semi-grateful recipients. The interest children show in each other's toys is the beginning of the interest felt between them as persons.

Functions of play

Stevenson (1965, pp. 30-5) describes five functions of the play of the 'ordinary' young child. These are abbreviated below, alongside a few ideas of Erikson (1950).

1. *Play acts as a bridge between reality and fantasy.* In learning about the 'real world' (the purpose and function of things) a child is less at the mercy of the unknown. Young children seem to perceive objects as having a life of their own, being capable of hitting back. Imagination is creative, but fantasies can be overwhelming unless balanced by reality.

2. The ordinary child works out in play *what the grownups' world is like*, and what it feels like to be grown up. There are traditional games of mothers and fathers, weddings, funerals and hospitals. The trying out of new roles helps children to establish their own identity.

3. Play is a means of *expressing strong feelings*: e.g., a little girl smacks her doll for being naughty, while anxious herself to conform. D. Winnicott (1957/64, p. 143) stresses that children need to be able to express aggression in a known environment without its retaliating or disintegrating.

4. The child in playing *learns various skills*—physical, intellectual and social. Erikson, in giving an example (p. 212) of the toddler building towers of bricks with a wish that he himself should knock the tower over, sees a connection with the child's efforts to stand and walk. 'It makes one feel stronger to know there is something weaker, and towers, unlike little sisters, can't cry and call mummy.'

5. Play is a means whereby the ordinary child *learns to share and to co-operate* with other children. Erikson says (p. 214) that at first other children are treated as things, while the child learns what content of play can be shared. But for quite a time, 'solitary play remains an indispensable harbour for the overhauling of shattered emotions after periods of rough going in the social seas'.

These functions of play may be seen as somewhat analogous to the classification of treatment methods worked out by Hollis (1964).

A developmental approach to the concept of play

A baby's world seems initially to consist of itself and its mother, bound up in an undifferentiated mass of feelings and sensations—some more comfortable than others. The comfortable experiences become associated with satisfaction and love; the uncomfortable with frustration, anger and the two-way anxiety about destructiveness. Gradually too, the baby begins to know his mother as a separate person, to become aware of his own boundaries, and his world begins to extend. His play centres first on his own body and then extends to available people and things. D. Winnicott (1957/64, p. 167) describes the stage where a small child may develop a pattern of sucking or stroking itself whilst holding a bit of cloth or whatever soft thing is chosen, thereby developing a relationship to an external object. Winnicott calls this a *transitional object*, because it represents the child's transition from being merged with the mother to becoming related to her as a separate person—the beginning of a relationship with the outside world. It is healthy to have such an object, though not all children need one. It (and its smell and texture) is very important to the child, particularly in times of stress. Winnicott sees it as the child's first possession or creation. The child needs to find his own first object, to which he may give a name; not to have it given, or taken away, but for it to be respected as something valuable which will gradually fade.

The distinction between the first object and later toys is not necessarily a sharp one, but the latter seem to be perceived by the child as increasingly separate from himself, as he grows surer of himself as a separate person. He grows more able to express himself through his toys, and tends to project many of his feelings of helplessness and inadequacy on to them. This emerges clearly in A. A. Milne's stories about Winnie-the-Pooh, where the animals go to ridiculous lengths in seeking to spare their own blushes and bolster their egos. The defence mechanisms of Pooh, Piglet and Eeyore entertain readers of all ages: all the characters are keenly, light-heartedly aware of each other's personalities, and Christopher Robin moves freely between the animals' (imaginary) world and his own, feeling more mature and powerful than they because he appreciates their weaknesses only too well. The last chapter is set in the Enchanted Forest: he and the animals have mixed feelings that he is becoming more independent and is about to leave them for school. But they reach an understanding that the Forest will still exist: that is, a promise of the continuing possibility of withdrawal and return between inner and outer reality, which can be a source of strength and refreshment.

Presumably Christopher Robin's interests would later extend to team games, perhaps a train set, stamp collecting, Cowboys and Indians ... Some of this would still be shared with his father but in a more obviously skilful, purposeful way. The ability to share toys and to take turns is learnt by experience; children of early school-age express rivalry with perhaps the least inhibition. The Opies' books (1959, 1969) illustrate a great range of children's games and occupations, many of them traditional. Millar (1968) writes eclectically on the psychology of play, and includes a section on group and gang activities. Eight- to twelve-year-olds prefer to play together; toys become less important than tools and realistic implements. Organised games with simple rules are later replaced by more complex games, sports and gang rivalries. The extent to which children congregate in gangs and continue to do so in adolescence is largely determined, Millar says, by the social, cultural and economic nature of the neighbourhood. She quotes Thrasher's gangs (1963) which were all in the slum districts of Chicago, and which had developed out of play-groups in crowded neighbourhoods. These gangs, typically with their specific secrets, rites and imitative customs, gave the individual a sense of belonging and of group solidarity against adults. In adverse conditions, the gangs were liable to become delinquent and their cohesiveness was strengthened by external hostility. Millar observes that the occupations of Thrasher's youths—brawling, fighting, sex, drinking, basket ball—are rather different from games of marbles or tag, and the youths' sexual maturity obviously influenced their activities. Young children (perhaps even Christopher Robin) naturally have their own version of sexual and aggressive games. Millar also discusses differences between the play of boys and girls, and between that of intelligent and retarded children.

Stories and painting pictures are an important content of play, both in early stages and later, when they probably gain in mundane realism. Melanie Klein's ideas (evaluated for social workers by Salzberger-Wittenburg in 1970) make some sense of the black and white world of childhood; the confusion between what actually happens and what is wished or feared, and the need to make reparation. Much of this is expressed in traditional fairy stories, peopled with good and bad parent-figures, witches, giants, dragons, kind and malicious fairies whose wishes and curses come true in concrete form, where the hero or heroine is engaged in a hazardous search for the good object and finally lives happily ever after.

As an alternative to the foregoing developmental approach, one might simply quote some poetry and prose by Rilke. First, from the 'Duino Elegies' (trans. Leishman and Spender):

> O hours of childhood,
> hours when behind the figures there was more
> than the mere past, and when what lay before us
> was not the future! We were growing, and sometimes
> impatient to grow up, half for the sake
> of those who'd nothing left but their grown-upness.
> Yet, when alone, we entertained ourselves
> with everlastingness: there we would stand,
> within the gap left between world and toy,
> upon a spot which, from the first beginning,
> had been established for a pure event.

Rilke enlarges elsewhere, in his lecture on Rodin and essay on Dolls, on the idea contained in his ninth line above ('within the gap left between world and toy'):

> If you can manage it, return with a portion of your weaned and grown-up feeling to any one of the things of your childhood with which you were much occupied. Consider whether there was anything closer ... and more necessary to you than such a Thing; whether everything —apart from it—was not in a position to hurt or wrong you, to frighten ... or confuse you with its uncertainty ... Was it not with a Thing that you first shared your little heart, like a piece of bread that had to suffice for two? ... This small forgotten object, that was ready to signify everything, made you intimate with thousands through playing a thousand parts, being animal and tree and King and child—and when it withdrew, they were all there. This Something, worthless as it was, prepared your relationships with the world, it guided

you into happening and among people, and, further: you experienced ... through its anyhow-appearance, through its enigmatic departure, all that is human, right into the depths of death.

So far, I have been thinking mainly about the play of 'ordinary children', all of whom are of course extraordinary in their individuality. It is typical of ordinary children to be importantly engrossed in their own activities, to be happily busy in a random sort of way, and perhaps to be day-dreaming to some purpose even when apparently doing nothing. Although the division between 'normal' and abnormal lies on a wavy dotted line, it is necessary now to consider

Children who may need some help through play

In the Yudkin report (1967, p. 20) a welfare clinic doctor comments on the obvious signs shown by children whose development is retarded, through lack of social experience and stimulation, even though their physical health may appear to be reasonably good. He describes the 6-10-months-old baby, 'whom one expects to be at the "I come, I see, I grab" stage', but who looks large-eyed at two coloured blocks on the table, with his hand held unnaturally in retreat behind the head. 'The older child, over 18 months of age, is often hyper-kinetic, flitting around the room, pulling down everything within reach, but failing to take an interest in any object, a sign of immaturity.' From this it appears that listless, aimless behaviour and over-activity without interludes of concentration are both signs of poor social development. Social workers meet many deprived children who find it difficult to play, lacking the means, motive and opportunity. There is an obvious value here in pre-school play-groups and clubs for school-age children, with scope also for workers to encourage opportunities within the children's own homes. Shapiro (1963) records the improvement which followed when students introduced play materials into the homes of 'non-coping mothers' whom they were visiting.

It seems, as Isaacs asserts (1948), that unhappy children play rather differently from those who are developing successfully and that, within the framework of a special relationship, they are able to convey the deeper sources of their troubles through play. It will be appropriate in the following chapter to distinguish further between playtherapy and casework with children; meanwhile C. Winnicott (1964, p. 45) makes a simple distinction between the psychotherapist, as a subjective figure in the child's world, and the social worker who 'starts off as a real person concerned with the external events and people in the child's life. In the course of her work with him she will attempt to bridge the gap between the external world and his feelings about it and in so doing she will enter his inner world too.' Here is part of a story told to a social worker by a five-year-old girl:

> There was a mother who had a clean house. There was a cat at the front door—outside but not inside, because her house was clean. There was a little boy outdoors but not indoors and the mother pushed the boy into the garden. Jack Frost was there and it was very cold. Also there was a mother doll and a baby boy pushed into the garden. Jack Frost was there and no green trees, only white. And all the people and Mrs Ladybird were in the garden ... and the Mother Ladybird was very worried and went very pale and pink, and wept tears round the apple pie. And they all ate the wet pie very uncomfortably ...'

This little girl and her circumstances are not known to me, but her message appears fairly clear: 'My mother seems to think more of her clean house (? and of my younger brother) than she does of me, and I feel pushed out into the cold. I invent lots of people to share with me the sterile loneliness outside. ? My mother should take warning from the ladybird in the nursery rhyme—"Your house is on fire and your children are gone." My mother seems unhappy too, blowing hot and cold—the situation is uncomfortable for all of us and the family food is sodden with sadness.' Few children could talk so directly of their plight, but the story speaks for itself.

Anxiety probably features in the play of all children, but play may be compulsive or repetitive if the anxiety is excessive. A thoughtful, permissive foster-mother was concerned that she had to stop a four-year-old boy from beating his golliwog for lengthy periods with a heavy saucepan—at first she thought he was 'getting something out of his system, but it grew worse and seemed to feed itself'. Possibly such behaviour could be expressed and contained more appropriately for a limited session in a psychiatric clinic setting. Play-therapy is possible, Erikson says (1950, p. 214) because children can be relied upon in a special environment to bring out 'whatever aspect of their ego has been ruffled most'. The child has the therapist and the toys temporarily to himself, without pressures from parents and siblings. He is free to choose how he spends the time, and some at least of the materials (dolls, soldiers, bricks, weapons, animals, sand, water, paints, etc.) will be evocative. Referral may have been for help with one or more of a range of problems such as enuresis, soiling, stealing, timidity, destructiveness, refusing food or school, slow learning at school or running away. The parent(s), in discussing the situation, may be helped to modify their interaction with the child. But the child himself usually cannot discuss his problems coherently, except in small snatches of conversation, and it is mainly through play that diagnosis and treatment is possible. Maclay (1970) gives an account of the therapist's methods in seeking to build a friendly relationship with children of various ages, and includes descriptions of the use individual children make of the sand tray and paintings in conveying their specific problems.

Young, apparently healthy children do not require direct treatment, though they may enjoy it; they are best helped indirectly through casework with the parents.

> Lyn, aged 3, was referred to the clinic by her mother because she was an only child who would not share her toys! It was the mother who needed short-term help, having set herself a standard of perfect motherhood, which prevented her from wanting any more children. In one of five interviews with a student social worker, she explained how she vetted the fairy stories carefully and thought it wrong to tell Lyn that the Big Bad Wolf was actually killed. When it was suggested to the mother that such stories impart knowledge to a child while the reality is still comfortably remote, and that learning of these things (particularly of birth and death) in the teens would be a shock, Lyn's mother recalled that this was exactly what had happened to *her*. To the next and final interview, Lyn brought a new doll with whom she was beginning to share most things. The interview turned into a tea-party for the doll, with mother, child and worker making plasticine food and teacups. The mother seemed more confident in her role, and suddenly wondered aloud whether to have a second baby soon.

The part adults play

The therapist may appear to play a very passive role, but treatment usually brings a measure of improvement and the child is more able to continue his own development from there. Axline (1966) tells the story of her warm relationship with Dibs, in which she responded less actively than some therapists would consider appropriate. A major function of the adult (whether psychotherapist, caseworker, parent or teacher) lies in providing a safe background for spontaneous play. The legal 'Place of Safety Order' can be compared with the much less traumatic, abstract place of safety provided by the child's daily play situation. Ingram (1961 a) discusses how residential workers may offer opportunities for play, making practical suggestions for the development of 'a living community with growing members'.

Social workers tend to have too much respect for the expertise of play-therapists to be tempted to trespass on their preserves, but I believe that some understanding of the significance of play would enable us to be more effective in the following areas of social casework:

1. It is useful to *observe* children's play when making a wider family assessment. For example, a little girl spent her time packing and unpacking a toy suitcase during the worker's initial home visit. It transpired that her mother had deserted and returned a few weeks earlier.
2. Play, drawings and stories are often the best means of *communicating* with children in situations where their words and ours are inadequate, and they need to discuss what is happening. Examples: a medical social worker drawing with a sick child in hospital; a probation officer playing draughts with a monosyllabic youth; a child care worker recreating in play the family of a child received into care, and ensuring that children leaving home take some of their own toys and possessions with them (to take everything would imply a complete break).
3. Understanding the significance of play is *an aid to casework with adults*—partly in the sense that social work (and administration) contains an element of 'playing with ideas'; mainly in that one becomes more aware of the symbolic meaning for clients of material objects such as money, food, roof, clothes, and there-

fore more able to work at an emotional level while simultaneously meeting important material needs. Also, deprived adults may need their own opportunities for recreation. Bond (1969) describes an F S U fathers' group which unexpectedly turned itself into the equivalent of a play-group.

This chapter has moved into a consideration of ways of communicating with children, and the theme continues into the next chapter about working directly with children.

3

Casework with children

I was set down from the carrier's cart at the age of
three; and there ... my life in the village began. The
June grass, amongst which I stood, was taller than I
was, and I wept ... For the first time in my life I was
alone in a world whose behaviour I could neither predict
nor fathom: a world of birds that squealed, of plants
that stank, of insects that sprang about without warning. I was lost and I did not expect to be found again.
I put back my head and howled, and the sun hit me
smartly in the face, like a bully. From this daylight
nightmare I was wakened, as from many another, by the
appearance of my sisters ...

(Laurie Lee: *Cider with Rosie*)

'She noticed that Dennis looked ill and frightened,
answered questions nervously and did not look up ...
She learned that Dennis was enuretic ...'
(Extract from a report on the circumstances leading to
the death of Dennis O'Neill in January 1945)

This chapter continues the theme of communication with
children: *first* looking at ways of meeting children with
and without words; *secondly* illustrating some of these
ways through a case record, and *thirdly* considering in

what kinds of situation it is appropriate to work directly with children. Casework, with its interwoven components of diagnosis and treatment, is not possible unless the client (of any age) and worker together are able to find some means of communication. Tod (1968 a, p. 111) defines communication as a reciprocal giving and receiving of both thoughts and feelings.

Surprisingly little of explicit, immediate relevance to social workers has been written on communication, and what has been formulated tends to fall into three groups. First, research papers in the psychology and sociology journals, often treating the subject in a highly academic manner, but sometimes triggering off practical ideas. At this level one might read Piaget (1959) on the language and thought of the child, or Beard's outline of Piaget's work (1969); Bernstein (1970 and earlier), Argyle (1967, extended in 1969), or more condensed theory in Mussen (1963) and Muller (1969). At the other extreme, some non-technical books have been produced for parent-figures, which may be more useful for social workers to read as an aid to jargon-free discussion with caretakers of their specific communication difficulties. Ginott's first two chapters (1965) on conversing with children contain potentially helpful advice—e.g. on how to avoid fruitless arguments by listening for the meaning underlying the child's stubborn assertions; how to offer unpressurising praise through making verbal response to the actual achievement rather than to the personality of the achiever. D. Winnicott (1957/64) conveys the things he believes mothers know instinctively in relationship with their babies, thus giving the 'good enough' mother freedom to follow her own path. Workers who grow wearily exasperated in trying to convey to caretakers that uprooted children do not thrive best with 'a clean break', may be refreshed to see how Stevenson (1965) explains our ideas untheoretically with clarity and conviction. D. Winnicott and Stevenson overlap with the middle range (or second level) of material directly relevant to social workers: C. Winnicott's printed talks (1964, 1968) are essential reading, supplemented by two chapters of Timms (1962/69) on casework with children and adolescents, Rich (1968) on interviewing children, Vann (1971), J. McWhinnie (1969), Dockar Drysdale's collected papers (1968), Konopka and other contributors to the series edited by Tod (1968, 1971).

Ideas about the use of language may be stimulated and explored by dipping into the literature at the three levels described above—i.e. the academic; the material produced specifically for social workers; and the practical suggestions offered to parent-figures. It might be worthwhile to begin by looking at one idea on all three levels. It is accepted in practice for instance that there is value in finding out a young child's daily-routine words before he leaves his family; similarly that when the care of an immigrant toddler is distributed between people of different cultures he is likely to have additional speech difficulties—but Bernstein introduces an academic dimension into such common sense. Bernstein has studied the sociological implications of language for some years, and a recently-produced paper (1970) is on 'restricted and elaborated codes'. He regards the latter as *person* rather than *status* orientated, whereas a restricted code depends on shared social assumptions, found for example within certain social strata/closed communities/peer groups of children. What is actually said in a restricted code 'is impersonal in the sense that the verbal component comes pre-packed', though the words can be augmented by non-verbal signs so that the whole enables a kind of shorthand between people who know each other well or who share clear-cut frames of reference. (Examples of mothers speaking in these two codes: 'shut your row'; 'what about playing outside now, dear, because you're getting on mummy's nerves'—

either could come as a surprise though the meaning of both is similar.)

Bernstein suggests that children socialised within middle-class strata can be expected to possess both an elaborated and a restricted code, while children socialised within some sections of working-class strata can be expected to be limited to a restricted code. This has obvious implications for progress at school, and furthermore conveys a sense of the complex language barriers which may arise for a child in a new environment. At the second level of the same idea, C. Winnicott (1968, p. 66) writes about the development of words as symbols linking the infant with those outside himself; how the use of language will only go on developing if the primary needs of food and care continue to be met 'by the person who is the embodiment of the words', and about the danger that children in disrupted circumstances may lose the capacity for speech or chatter fluently but meaninglessly. And at the third level, Stevenson (1965, p. 60) explains the value of a foster-mother meeting a child in his own home beforehand so that she can talk with him about it during the fostering period.

Verbal and non-verbal communication

It is not always easy for grown-ups and children to converse, even casually in ordinary daily living sometimes, let alone in a formal interview situation. A child may have the gift of spontaneity once freed to talk naturally, but this can be outweighed by the considerable disadvantages of:

(a) limited vocabulary
(b) limited ability to conceptualise—particularly in terms of time and space
(c) confusion between the real and the imaginary, which makes fantasies rife and may result in 'telling lies'

46

(d) a peculiarly clear-cut form of logic which may lead to strange conclusions

(e) unformed defences which may be crystal-clear or singularly elusive

(f) lack of social poise which may cause dead silence, giggles or 'silly chatter'

(g) insufficient maturity to take responsibility for his own words and opinions

(h) a grasshopper mind which does not 'keep to the point'.

It must often seem to children as though adults have little desire to converse except when wanting to make their own point clear. As social workers we may pride ourselves on our willingness to spend time in speaking honestly with children, but we ourselves labour under extra disadvantages: that the material we have to discuss often makes for painful, puzzled listening, and that parent-figures commonly expect and try to manipulate us to talk *to* children (especially in terms of giving 'a good talking-to') rather than *with* them. And children are naturally unwilling to have painful home-truths forced upon them. They may appear to listen dutifully, and then ask a question which shows the worker's Greek words were wasted. A busy worker may respond by repeating his words very simply and clearly, and then disappear, hoping professional honour is satisfied. A further obstacle is that, in situations of stress and uncertainty, children tend to lose even the small amount of technical/social knowledge they had previously gained.

It could be argued that many adult clients are childish and/or child-like to the extent that it is difficult to sustain 'a normal conversation' with them. It is also true that even expert verbalisers can become incoherent under the pressure of personal problems, and that the most intelligent conceptualisers may use intellectualisation as a defence against feeling. So the problem of finding an appropriate

47

means of communication is not confined to social work with children, although it is characteristic of such work. It is also characteristic (as social interaction is vital for development) that children are extremely adept in managing to communicate when adults can adapt to a meaningful wave-length. Once both parties are tuned in, casework with children is much like casework with anybody else, except perhaps that a child is different in having very limited freedom of choice. With any client, there has to be a balance between recognising his needs and those of society, but a child is limited both by his dependence on adults and by his relative inability to distinguish between his *short-term wants* and his *long-term needs*. For example, he may need rather than want to have his tonsils removed, and again: one might rely on the judgment of a sixteen-year-old as he decides on his future employment and accommodation, but one cannot base a recommendation for adoption solely on the opinion of the six-year-old child directly concerned. This may only be another way of saying that children are at very great risk of having things done to them, either 'for their own good' or for our convenience. There is some parallel here with the idea of discipline for children consisting ideally of freedom within boundaries, and one hopes that the boundaries of law and administration, structuring the child's small measure of self-determination in casework, are designed and interpreted with care, integrity and imagination.

Methods of communication can be divided for theoretical convenience into those which are verbal and those which are non-verbal. The latter are more essential with very young children, whose healthy development implies that an increasing use of words is possible as they grow older, but non-verbal communication is relevant throughout life, particularly in times of stress. When children and adults talk together (and perhaps when any two people meet in an atmosphere of watchful constraint) direct words often take the form of question and answer. This can be helpful if the questions come naturally from the child and if the answers are clear, appropriate and repeated when necessary, but it is unfortunate when the adult is reduced to asking a battery of questions which evoke monosyllabic replies. Obviously it is sensible and practicable sometimes to ask questions, but a straight question tends to restrict freedom of response in a way that a comment does not. The bald question, 'Why do you steal?' certainly will not receive an enlightening reply. Much of a child's verbalisation will in any case be indirect; his own direct questions may contain hidden questions, and his remarks, though ostensibly about someone or something else, may be oblique references to himself: for example, later in this chapter, when Jenny, Rose and Peter talk about the dog, about people going to prison and about the worker living alone. The pressure of feeling, or the studied nonchalance, accompanying an indirect remark is sometimes a sign that it carries underlying meaning.

It is not particularly useful to categorise defences commonly employed by young children in their conversation, and I prefer to think of defences rather as Lazarus does (1966), in terms of reappraisal of information for internal or external publication. The following brief case example illustrates the use of direct and indirect verbal communication (plus some non-verbal) and shows how Henry reappraises an unpalatable fact. The worker here did not try to force Henry to look squarely at the facts: a helpful worker does not use forceful or cunning tactics in order to 'break down defences'; he merely hopes to help his client feel safe enough to become less guarded.

Henry, a thin, apathetic boy aged eight, was the only one of five siblings to need statutory care for ten days. His mother had deserted the family on a Wednesday; Henry was in the midst of his father's plans to place most of the children privately with relatives, and he himself was the last child to leave home on the Friday night. He refused to bring any toys with him to the foster-home, nor was he comforted by his half-drunk father's final embrace and promises never to forget him. (Such promises would immediately imply the possibility of being forgotten.) He did not talk to the worker, who imagined he was bound to have exact knowledge of the whereabouts of his brothers and sisters. On the following Monday, he turned to the worker with a very puckered face and asked, 'Have the four little ones gone to a Home?' The worker replied no, they had gone to his aunts in the next town, and that it was perhaps better for them to go to people they knew, because they were too little to understand. The worker added that it was hard too for him to understand, but he was bigger than the four little ones and perhaps the foster-parents were not such strangers now as they had seemed on Friday. Henry thought this over and then said, 'My Dad wanted *me* to go to my Auntie Betty's for a holiday, but I said no, because I said the four little ones must go, because they are too young to understand and must go to someone they know.' He seemed relieved to have twisted the decision, for him alone to be received into care, into being his own choice rather than have it imply rejection by his family. He needed to repeat this conversation a week later on his journey back home.

Child care history might have been different if Dennis O'Neill had made a direct statement of complaint to the official visitor, but his silent fear and unhappiness (as quoted at the beginning of this chapter) was in itself a communication that something was wrong. Non-verbal communications occur and interact in a vast range of signs, facial expressions, gestures and poses, actions and behaviour. An adolescent girl talked with relaxed, superficial friendliness during an interview, but her half-hidden foot was silently tapping madly—wanting to be on its way to an evening with the boy friend? I once attended a lecture on communication with children and was disappointed to find it entirely about numerous behaviour problems such as enuresis, but took the point that such problems are in themselves a very real communication from the child. Stories, drawings and play are frequently used more creatively by children, giving another opportunity for the adult to respond within the same focus.

A worker visited a brother and sister aged seven and six in residential care, in order to break the news that their mother, who had earlier arranged to reclaim them the following week, had started a new cohabitation and no longer wanted them. The worker dreaded the effect of his news, had rehearsed carefully beforehand the kindest way of phrasing it, but was taken aback when the children showed no reaction whatsoever. His lame explanations died into silence ... after a pause one of the children suggested that the worker should help them do a jig-saw puzzle. He joined in rather hopelessly, seeing the puzzle as a distraction to the job in hand. In fact the puzzle was probably the children's way of asking for help in sorting out the disintegrated pieces of their own circumstances, and he could have used it as such by keeping the subject open for discussion while focusing on the jig-saw puzzle.

Children do always react in some way, even if simply by sitting numb, so the worker needs to be sensitively aware of the child's choice of medium and to respond accordingly. It is very important not to anticipate the desired reaction, but to await, observe and *meet the child's actual response*. Dockar Drysdale (1968, p. 31) writes of the potential danger of intuitive communication used by a disturbed adult to create a kind of no-man's-land between adult and child, which is liable to be harmful to the child 'because he may become the one who has to produce the correct responses; lacking resources and a clear boundary to his inner world, he may be exploited by mother or worker, who will be unaware of the harm being done. Intuition informed is an essential tool: intuition uninformed can be a dangerous weapon.' (A research paper by Lennard, Beaulieu and Embrey, 1970, about communication systems in families containing a schizophrenic child, showed a tendency for the mothers to communicate with their adult schizophrenic sons less in factual terms than in inter-personal terms flavoured by 'a controlling, intrusive and projective quality'.) Young children, and older children in disrupted circumstances, certainly need help from safe adults in order for them to know what they are feeling: the necessary safeguards lie in the adult's willingness to create a favourable climate in which communication can take place, and then to wait in a receptive, reliable manner so as to be ready to try to understand and to respond to a *real* message whether or not it is garbled or in semaphore.

With the same idea of creating a safe neutral area in which to enable helpful communication, C. Winnicott (1964, p. 50) writes of the value of 'a third thing' in casework with children. This third thing may be concrete or abstract: a photograph, car-ride, toy, joke, animal, story, letter, game, map ... it may be an end in itself by making the necessary communication without words, or it may be used jointly as a focus for conversation. Here is an example of two imaginary workers, Miss X and Mr Y, each attempting to talk with a child in residential care through focusing on the child's drawing. There is no need for them to possess the expertise necessary to *interpret* the content of the drawing: child and worker simply use it as a talking point. Mr Y speaks with quiet, friendly matter-of-factness, making far less obvious effort than Miss X, but achieving more in that he lets the picture and its meaning emerge from the child. (Of course one brief verbal exchange will not produce startling results for good or ill, and the examples would be part of a series of conversations.)

Miss X: 'That's a lovely drawing—what is it?'

Child: 'It's our house'

Miss X: 'Which house do you mean? Auntie and Uncle's house?'

Child: ... (*short pause*)

Miss X: 'I expect it is, because that's where you live now, isn't it? And Mummy hasn't got a house yet, has she?'

Child: 'Mum says she's going to build us a house, when she's got enough bricks ...'

Miss X: 'Yes, but you're staying here until then—it takes a lot of bricks to build a house ... You've drawn Uncle busy in the garden, and Auntie hanging out the clothes ... You *like* it here, don't you?'

Child: 'Yes ... I don't know ...'

Communication breaks down, with sullen child and floundering adult. Here is Mr Y, who uses comments rather than questions.

Mr Y: 'Tell me about your drawing ...'

Child: 'It's our house ... the house where *I* live ...'

Mr Y: 'The house where *you* live ...'

Child: 'With Mum and Dad and our Yvonne and Gary and Kim and June and the babies ...'

Mr Y: '... all together ...'

Child: 'Yes, but we don't live there now ...'

Mr Y: 'That's sad—you'd like to live all together again ...'

Child: 'Mum says she's going to build us a house—when she's got enough bricks ... Dad's digging in the garden—he's going to grow things ...'

Mr Y: 'For you to eat ...'

Child: 'Yes, chips off of potatoes—no cabbage—I don't like Auntie's cabbage ...'

Mr Y: 'You like your mother's food best ...'

Child: 'Uncle says Auntie's a lovely cook ... but ...'

Mr Y: 'But food tastes nicer in your own home ...'

Child: (*continues to talk*)

The second conversation is obviously more honest than the first (partly because Miss X was so anxious for the child to be happy that she gave no opportunity for the real identity of the objects in the drawing ever to emerge; perhaps she was taught always to emphasise the reality-situation, and has forgotten the reality of fantasy) but what if anything did Mr Y achieve? First, the conversation enabled him to *assess* the child's preoccupation with memories of the past and hopes of future reunion. One could very well have guessed this, though children away from home may rarely mention their own families unless opportunities are provided. Secondly, the conversation assisted in *treatment*, in that Mr Y accepted the child's longing to be back with his own family, his sense of loss and uncertainty, and his resentment of his present circumstances even though he is receiving good care. One cannot order a person so to arrange his feelings that he forgets the past, resigns himself to the present and awaits the future patiently. But Mr Y's conversation will have helped the child to achieve some perspective on his life as a whole; to be more in touch with his feelings, and in fact to become more settled away from home—more accepting of the housemother now that eating her food no longer implies disloyalty to his own parents.

If children in need of 'special care' are to begin to let themselves take other than superficially the care that is offered, they must be allowed to express to someone the very real and painful feelings they have about being in circumstances which stigmatise them as different and perhaps as unlovable. They cannot merely be coaxed, browbeaten, teased or jollied along into making the best of shattering events. The pressure of fear, anger and bewilderment is surely only increased in stricken children who find themselves surrounded by a conspiracy of determined cheerfulness. When a toddler falls headlong, it is noticeable how, in those breathless seconds between fall and subsequent yelling, grown-ups often laugh in order to show the child that he is not hurt. I am not suggesting he should deliberately be encouraged to cry, but that he should have freedom to find out for himself whether or not his fall was funny, and that comfort should be available if he seeks it. Tears and laughter are sometimes interchangeable as tension-relievers—both are therapeutic; laughter calls for concern rather than collusion when it clearly arises from pressure of distress. For example, a physically handicapped child may clown defiantly so as to gain some sense of control over the way he fears other people may perceive him, and one might more appropriately regard his antics with gentle affection than with embarrassed mirth.

Stevenson (1963) writes about the caseworker's helpful willingness to tolerate tears, and Konopka (1968, pp. 88-92) describes three pre-requisites to communication with adolescent girls in institutions: listening, observing, empathising. Perhaps it is the worker's empathy which tells him when a child wants physical comfort—again this could be off-putting from a comparative stranger or if it is motivated by the worker's own need to demonstrate affection: a mixture of spontaneous discretion is necessary if physical holding is to be acceptably meaningful. Apart from the non-verbal communication of literally holding a distressed child, there are many ways of symbolising encircling warmth—one possibility is to keep a rug in the car. Children certainly understand such symbols: one little boy asked his worker (who had supported him through several painful situations) to give him and his sisters a piece of elastoplast each as a good-bye present, 'in case we get hurt'.

Case record as illustration

This record (*with my comments in italics*) covers a short period in the lives of Mr and Mrs Lane's three unrelated foster-children:

JENNY: aged twelve, illegitimate, received into care at two years old, and placed initially in a Home for health reasons. Her first foster-mother died when she was seven, the second soon became ill, and Jenny came to live with the Lanes four years ago. Jenny's mother lost contact after her marriage two years ago. Jenny is of low intelligence, has prolonged sulks interspersed with irritating 'helpfulness' and servility, and is jealous of the other children. Recently Mrs Lane was very upset to discover that Jenny is stealing small things from her; hoarding these plus accumulations of 'rubbish' and eating 'unnecessary food' in bed. Stealing was the 'one thing (Mrs Lane) could not stand', and she wanted it stopped quickly.

ROSE: aged eight, placed here three years ago from her own multi-problem family at the request of a psychiatrist who took a serious view of her withdrawn and somewhat bizarre behaviour. There have been ups and downs with Rose, but on the whole she was holding her own.

PETER: aged six, brought up by Mr and Mrs Lane from early babyhood, and feeling like their own. He was born into a large family which never knew itself as a family, being split up even while it was growing. Peter had a poor start with bad health, and has been slow in his development.

FOSTER-HOME: Geographically isolated, reliable, easygoing, revolving round foster-children, of whom Mrs Lane 'could never have enough'—a kindly, garrulous woman. Mr Lane kept himself (or was kept) in the shade. Their own children are nearly grown up, and away from home.

15th February   I took over the supervision of this

foster-home three weeks ago. I called today to drive
Jenny and Mrs Lane to a quickly arranged child guidance
appointment at Mrs Lane's wish. (*We are not told
whether Jenny had previously had treatment or how
much the worker had discussed the problem with Mrs
Lane. The new worker seems to be responding mainly
to Mrs Lane's sense of urgency about the stealing, and
may be trying to appease Mrs Lane for her recent loss
of the former well-known worker. Also Mrs Lane will
possibly feel less 'loyalty' to a new worker, and
therefore less guilt in asking for Jenny's removal now.*)
Mrs Lane was feeling ill, but was so anxious about the
stealing that she was determined to come too. I
persuaded her not to, saying I would put her point of
view and go again with her later. Finding on the
journey that Jenny did not know why we were going,
I told her that Mrs Lane was worried about the things
Jenny was taking from her; that we were going today to
try to understand more about it and to see how we
can help. Jenny said nothing to this, but continued
to chat pleasantly of other things. (*Presumably Jenny
was not unaware of the reason for the journey, but
finds it too difficult to talk about.*) She seemed to enjoy
the afternoon's outing and the appointment, where
various suggestions were pooled with the aim of
maintaining the foster-home. I told Mrs Lane briefly
about it on our return, offering to discuss it fully when
she was better. I saw the other children briefly.

18th February   Mrs Lane had developed a serious
illness and was admitted to hospital this morning. It
had been arranged that foster-relatives, living about
thirty miles away in more comfortable financial
circumstances, should have the children until she was
fit. The children were excited with a mixture of anxiety
and holiday spirits, but confident about going to people
they know well. Jenny sat in the front seat of the
car, because of being the eldest, and complained of a
bad headache, but was keen to show responsibility for
the others. Mr Lane was also at the hospital and I had
collected the children from a neighbour. As we left,

they were worried about the Lanes' dog, left alone in the house. (*The children's concern about the dog seems to be an indirect communication of their own anxiety about themselves.*) I said it was difficult for the dog to understand, but Mr Lane would soon be back, and Mr and Mrs Lane had made the best plans they could for everybody. (*Workers vary in whether they reply directly or indirectly—it is useful to reply at least partially in the terms presented.*)

I felt most concerned about Jenny, with this upset coming on top of her stealing. (*But it is not easy to meet Jenny's likely feeling that she has somehow harmed Mrs Lane, or taken too much from her in her own desperation to get enough for herself, or that Mrs Lane has perhaps deserted her as a punishment.*) She and I agreed that Mrs Lane would be relieved to feel Jenny was there to help. (*The worker knows Jenny has a need to be helpful, and it may be all right to encourage Jenny in this way, unless it adds extra pressure or implies that she is not valued except for her usefulness.*) We all agreed we felt sad about Mrs Lane being in hospital. I suggested ways in which they could keep in touch with messages and letters (*a valuable life-line to prevent their feeling quite cut off*), and Jenny said Mrs Lane got better very quickly last time she had bronchitis (? *denying her fear that she may lose a third foster-mother through illness*). Mostly we had to concentrate on Peter's endless questions, delivered in a high, piping voice. Squashing Peter, who is used to it, and is aware of being Mrs Lane's favourite, was an outlet for Jenny and Rose's anxiety, although they were equally eager to hear the answers to the questions. (*The two girls use Peter as their spokesman-cum-scapegoat; he is perhaps asking things they would like to ask but feel would be inappropriate at their age. If Peter asks 'endless questions', he may be too het up to hear replies, and is simply driven on by the one question he dare not ask.*)

Rose was quiet at first, but later grew agitated when other cars followed us, calling out to them that they were copy-cats, and cheaters if they passed us. She explained to me that she was frightened of following cars bumping into us. (*This fear on the road is typical of deprived/disturbed children—a fear perhaps of other people's hostility and of their own aggression turned inwards. Also cars symbolise power, autonomy and speed, and thus emphasise the children's own feelings of helplessness in coping with circumstances over which they have no control. Workers vary in whether they consider a car a suitable setting for casework: some feel they should simply concentrate on their driving. I think a car journey is a good time for communication because people often talk more freely when sitting side by side than face to face; also it may be easier to talk about the two places at each end of the journey when one is travelling between them, and thirdly the client may easily change the subject if he wishes by pointing out some passing object of interest.*) Later Rose nursed Peter's large teddy-bear and held a three-cornered conversation with me and the bear, having explained to me first that the gruff voice was Teddy's. (*Here Rose is using 'a third thing' again, and she possibly hopes to be more acceptable through using a possession of the favoured Peter's as her medium. Rose has quite a vivid imagination, but seems to be trying to keep it in balance by explaining things to the worker.*) Teddy did not have anything very special to say, and seemed mainly to be practising his voice.

I mentioned the children's previous caseworker, who has recently left to have a baby. (*Another link with the past. Rose seems less sure of herself in conversation than the other two.*) They wanted to know whether I too am having a baby, and if not why not. (*? Partly sexual curiosity and partly wondering whether they can count on the new worker continuing with them.*) We pursued the subject quite a bit further though the girls felt Peter's interest to be extreme. (*This might have been an opportunity to speak of the children's individual family backgrounds.*) They are all tending to be extra moral with each other in spasms, and I think

Jenny's stealing and Mrs Lane's attitude to it has jolted them all. (*They would probably all three be unsettled through awareness of the danger of Jenny's behaviour resulting in her permanent removal from the foster-home.*) Peter has a pretend-grandmother, who is able to live in any little tumbledown cottage in the wilds of the country that we happened to see. (*Apparently Peter does not visualise members of his own broken family inhabiting ordinary houses in a town. If he has no concrete knowledge of a grandmother, he might equally well imagine her living in great luxury, as fantasies tend to be extreme.*) They seemed reasonably settled by the time I left them with the foster-relatives, though Peter was tearful at first.

Mrs Lane died early the next day. The children were told by the foster-relatives, who were upset because Jenny, although the most tearful, had shown immediate concern about her own possessions in the foster-home. Rose and Peter could hardly grasp the news. The relatives were too distressed to keep the children many days, and the children were prepared for the idea of the Reception Centre. None of them has been there before. (*The children's worst fears are confirmed when Mrs Lane deserts them by dying. All of them have been 'bereaved' at least once before, and Jenny four times — so she is naturally preoccupied with the symbol of her own small possessions. Unfortunately her apparent callousness offends the relatives, who may feel that the strain of having foster-children has contributed to Mrs Lane's death. Grief reactions may include shock, depression, hostility, and the need to blame someone, so the foster-children are an obvious target, and they of course interact with their own renewed grief reactions. Whereas children in an ordinary family do not normally lose their entire home when one parent dies, this often happens to foster-children, especially if they were not originally wanted whole-heartedly by the bereaved partner. Local authority care unfortunately does not provide the infallibly safe place the public likes to think it does, when care is initially requested.*)

23rd February   The previous caseworker and I
attended Mrs Lane's funeral. There seemed to be no
question of the children going. Afterwards we talked
with the relatives, and with Mr Lane who seemed quite
broken up. (*Presumably the workers attend the funeral
partly in recognition of Mrs Lane's service to the department, and partly in order to be able to tell the children
about it afterwards.*)

24th February   I went early this morning to Mr
Lane's home to collect all the children's clothes, toys
and possessions, as he could not bear to see these lying
about. I spent a bit of time with him, first listening to
his distress, and then gradually felt my way towards
seeing whether he will have much interest in the
children in future. (*It seems to be tacitly accepted that
Mr Lane's shadowy role as foster-father is finished. So
he is likely to opt out completely now, but the three
children have regarded him as a father-figure, and the
worker hopes he may be helped to show at least a very
small continuing interest in them.*) I drove straight on
for the children, because the relatives felt unable to
keep them any longer, and the Reception Centre would
not be ready to receive them until afternoon, so it meant
my marking time with the children between the two
places for three hours. This turned out to be a good
thing, as the children had a lot needing to be talked
about, and they welcomed the longer breathing-space.
(*The worker had been privately angry, when trying
to make these arrangements beforehand by telephone,
to find that the three groups of parent-substitutes
could not synchronise in streamlining the children's
move. Her distress was partly, she thought, because the
situation highlighted the extreme vulnerability of
foster-children in general, and mainly because she
dreaded having to spend three hours in such painful
circumstances.*) It was impossible to have more than
a stilted leave-taking of the foster-relatives, and only
Jenny was tearful. The week there cannot have been
easy, although of course the children did not say so.
(*It is remarkable how few complaints foster-children*

typically do make—possibly they feel to be in an insufficiently secure position.)

I took them out to lunch in a café, where we caused quite a diversion with our long, unconventional meal. Jenny kept clearing the table for the waitress, and they all seemed emotionally hungry, whilst reminding each other in a pathetic, manipulative way that I am not their mother and therefore could not really be expected to provide all the food they wanted —and had, within sickness limits. (*The children are in limbo these three hours, having just left the last known place, and they seem to be turning to the worker as a temporary mother-figure who is giving them 'food' while they prepare for the next step. The café, like a car, is a place of transit.*) Peter announced loudly in the middle of lunch: 'Mummy is dead, and under the ground'. We talked a bit about Mrs Lane and her funeral, though only Jenny begins to realise the finality yet. (*Peter's remark is 'embarrassing in public' and might have seemed unfeeling to the relatives, but presumably he is just trying out his blind idea aloud, to see how it sounds, and whether it can possibly be true.*) They asked about other foster-relatives, and their foster-home, and whether the dog and the furniture were still there. I said the dog was sad and doesn't quite understand what has happened; the furniture is still there, and Mr Lane will look after the dog but can do no more, because of having to go out to work. (*Children sometimes find it hard to believe that a place still exists, after it has been lost to them personally. It must seem hard to these three that the dog is kept when they are not.*)

I made up the sort of message Mr Lane might have sent them if he had been fit to, and gave them some real messages from other people they know, which pleased them—except for one from a girl whom they said they didn't like because she had not kept her own baby. (*They may be feeling that they wouldn't be in their present predicament if their own parents had kept them. This would have been another chance for the worker to help them sort out their earlier circumstances, but probably she feels there are enough immediate issues.)* We had a second discussion about babies. Jenny said she hoped to marry and have four children, two boys and two girls, and then she would bring them to see me in my little flat. *(Jenny is naturally dreaming ahead to a time when she can rely on a home of her own.)* They had wanted before to know where I live, and Jenny seemed concerned now that I live alone. She said, 'Whatever do you do? Do you talk to yourself?' I replied lightly in terms of being quite all right, and then answered Peter's question 'Shall we come to live with you?', by saying it would be very nice, but I go out to work like Mr Lane. Later Jenny showed similar concern about my having to drive some distance back to the area office by myself: 'Whatever will you do? Will you talk to yourself?', and I realised then she was speaking of her own fear of being alone, so was able to explain carefully that she herself will certainly have someone to live with and to look after her as long as she wants. *(Fortunately clients usually give a second chance for the listener to tune in. It is just possible also that Jenny's remark shows anxiety over her recent psychiatric appointment—i.e. a fear that she is 'mental' and may 'talk to herself'.)* Rose was quieter than the other two, but suddenly said, 'Isn't it right that people who steal are sent to prison?' I said grown-ups sometimes are for a time but never children. *(The three hours seem to be dividing naturally into two: first about the recent past, and now the children are beginning to show anxiety about where they are going next. They may have some fear of going to 'a place for naughty children'.)*

We drove past the Reception Centre after lunch, just to see where it was and what it looked like, and then went on for a couple of miles. Peter did not mention his pretend-grandmother today. I said he will now be nearer his favourite elder brother and will be able to see him again soon. We stopped in a lane, and had some sweets before turning back. They asked innumerable questions about the Reception Centre and the people there, and whether they would like it, and whether I liked it and had ever lived there, and what would happen next. (*Some of the pressure underlying these questions might have been eased if the worker had acknowledged more openly the children's sense of loss and confusion.*) They learnt the names of the staff, and were especially keen to know whether the staff and I like children, and whether any of us prefer boys to girls. Peter said firmly, 'I am going to like it, even if the girls don't!' Jenny and Rose were annoyed with him, and told me quite heatedly that Peter often showed off, by saying Mrs Lane liked him better than them—they added that this was true. I said even if it were true, I knew that Mrs Lane had loved them all, and most people like boys and girls equally much, though a few cannot help liking girls best or boys best. (*Peter of course is afraid of not liking the new place when he asserts the opposite. It would not have helped if the worker had tried to convince them falsely that Mrs Lane had had no favourite. Each of the three is so vulnerable that they are a threat to each other as well as a support in trouble.*) They were keen to know if they could do just as they liked in the next place, and I explained that they could within reason, and the staff would be friendly, and Rose could ask for her customary night-light, and the staff would welcome Jenny's help. This seemed to be a slight turning-point for Jenny.

They seemed relieved rather than resentful that the car was crammed with their belongings. As we went up the drive eventually, they volunteered that they were 'a bit scared' but thought it was 'going to be all right'. (*They are probably putting the best possible face on it, and haven't expressed much direct grief today, but the remark does show a healthy balance between extremes of apprehension and unnatural aplomb. They would not have achieved this small measure of confidence on a quick silent journey from one place to the next.*) They were impressed to find that the staff knew their names and something about them, and vice versa. (*It helps their sense of identity to be known on sight, and it will be reassuring too if the residential staff and the fieldworker meet in a friendly way.*) Their arrival was eased by sorting their things which they were pleased to see again after six days. They seemed to be settling by the time I left, having promised to come again soon, though Peter was rather desperately immersed in his toys, with eyes full of tears. Jenny and Rose were interested in the kitchen preparations for tea. (*Not through childish greed, but needing practical assurance that life will go on.*)

This record covers only an end and a beginning. The residential staff and the fieldworker will play complementary roles in helping the three children continue to make some coherence of past, present and future. At case conferences there will perhaps be mention of Jenny continuing to steal, Rose being withdrawn and Peter having nightmares. It will be debated whether they need to be treated as a trio of foster-siblings or as individuals while new plans are made, and whether their future needs will best be met in one or more of whichever foster-homes/community homes are available; also whether it will be helpful for them to see more of their own relatives (whom they do not seem to regard with any open hope of salvation) during this interim period. There will be months of work ahead before we can visualise them beginning to settle elsewhere.

When is it appropriate to offer children casework help?

Social workers vary in whether they consider it their function to work directly with children, or whether they believe it preferable to concentrate on helping parent-figures to help the children with whom they live. Convincing arguments exist for both viewpoints, and it may be that both are valid, depending on specific circumstances. Some of the arguments rely on common sense, some on imagination, and for some it is necessary to distinguish between casework and residential work, and between casework and psychotherapy.

One of the saddest aspects of Jenny, Rose and Peter's situation (an extreme situation which is far from being unique) was that they really had no parent-figure available to help them through their crisis: their closest adult, Mrs Lane, had died; Mr Lane and the foster-relatives were immersed in their own grief to the exclusion of the children, and their natural parents were not in close contact nor would it have been easy for them to give comfort for the loss of a foster-mother who only entered the children's lives because of the parents' own failure. So it seems the caseworker was the best person available; also she represented the agency which the children knew to be responsible for their care and, though it is humiliating to be dependent on public care, the department itself is sufficiently inhuman to remain alive whilst simultaneously discharging its responsibilities through the medium of human beings. Certainly there is a definite place for direct communication with children during *separation experiences* and in *crisis-situations*, when the child's own adults may be *hors de combat*. Backing this argument is the fact that workers become fairly accustomed to disruptive situations, and have some knowledge of crisis theory (Caplan, 1961; papers edited by Parad, 1965) so are in a good position to offer skilled, reliable help.

On the other hand one could argue that if the department had concentrated on selecting and maintaining reliable foster-parents in reasonably good health, it might not have exposed the three children to the risk of losing Mrs Lane. Or the worker might conceivably have used her crisis theory to help Mr Lane and the foster-relatives to work through their grief to a point where they had something concrete to offer the children. Again, perhaps the natural parents were too easily overlooked. If they had been kept in closer contact, might they not have risen to this tragic situation? If one uses the same reasoning as Kirk (1964), in terms of adopters needing to mourn their own childlessness in order subsequently to identify with their adopted child in helping him to deal with the loss of his biological parents, might not 'a failed parent' develop enough empathy to comfort his own child who is now a bereaved foster-child? None of these speculations affects the fact that our particular worker was probably best placed to meet the three children's immediate need, and my point here is that workers may sometimes under-estimate the potential contribution of other interested parties. There may be some danger of workers under-mining the relationship between children and parent-figures who offer *the daily care* which is more essential than casework help. Child care workers rightly place great value on being the link between child, parent and care-taker, and the link between past, present and future, but there are slight indications (for instance in George's re-search, 1970) that this extremely positive function is sometimes so closely guarded that the link-making abili-ties of caretakers in daily touch with the child are ignored.

A worker's own motivations have considerable effect on the emphasis given to contrasting aspects of the work. In general terms we are all interested in the well-being of children and families, but any one individual may be slan-ted towards an identification with children in trouble, or similarly towards the needs of parent-figures. Whatever the personal slant (and one safeguard lies in being aware of it) there is much suffering to meet, and some people find it more distressing to be open to the pain of children than to that of adults. (Other workers may wish to escape from the ingrained hostility and intractability of awkward adults to the comparative pleasure found in children's company.) Possibly some of the arguments used for not offering casework help to children are rationalisations to protect us from too much direct contact with bewildered, withdrawn or defiant young victims of chronically unhappy situations. C. Winnicott (1964, p. 43) suggests that we need to be aware of the strength of our own feelings about the suffering of children; that we can be overwhelmed by seeing the gaps in children's lives, and are therefore tempted to concentrate on filling these gaps 'at the expense of the other part of our job which is to look at the gaps with him'. She sees the capacity to suffer as a sign of health and a growing-point in the individual, and believes that we need to be more aware of the suffering behind our clients' hostility.

This perhaps leads to another argument in favour of working directly with children : that the worker occupies a more neutral less vulnerable position than a parent-figure and so is a safer person to receive the inevitable hostility and negative behaviour of children in difficulties (particularly of adolescents who confide less in the adults with whom they live, and of children who are temporarily beyond the understanding acceptance of their caretakers). Is it asking too much of foster-parents that they should 'accept the suffering' which may cause, for example, constant wet beds and daily washing of sheets, or that an over-worked housemother should try dispassionately to understand why her food is wolfed or spurned? Might the mother of a physically handicapped child feel too guilty about her imperfect creation of her own image to bear the direct expression of the child's natural resentment?

The above argument: that a fieldworker is better able to accept a child's negative feelings without 'taking it personally', without being hurt or retaliatory, needs to be examined in relation to the role of caretakers including residential staff. C. Winnicott (1964, p. 30) makes a clear distinction between casework and residential work whilst regarding both as valuable methods of treatment:

> Children need from the residential worker something direct and real, and treatment surely lies in the worker's ability to provide for them real experiences of good care, comfort and control. This good care will include timing that can allow personal experiences to be completed and a sense of achievement attained. It will include recognising that each child has individual needs, and attempting to meet the needs of each if only in a token way. The token can be used because behind it is both the recognition of the need and the will to meet it.

The *time element* is important because communication with children means waiting for opportunities: the most fortunate caseworker is unlikely to have more than an hour a week available regularly for such waiting (and an hour a week probably feels less supportive to a child than it does to an adult client) whereas the caretaker has day-long chances for spontaneous conversation which make her words meaningful as a natural part of the complete pattern of care. Holman (1964) pleads for more time for fieldworkers if they are to meet children on other than crisis-occasions, and in a subsequent article (1966) he provides some evidence to show that children in care may have surprisingly positive ideas about the funct ons of their own caseworker: e.g., 'He has helped me. I wouldn't know how much, just seeing me, I don't know how it helps, but it does.'

It is notoriously difficult to formulate definitions of casework (see Timms 1964, pp. 2-5) but might one simply term one aspect of it a method of helping people in their personal relationships? When children are insecure in their relationships, whether at home or elsewhere, it places mounting strain on those (of any age) directly involved. In so far as casework is a way of helping these people with their pressure of feeling about each other and about the situation, I believe it is a valid method which ideally should be available to everybody concerned, including children and their parent-figures separately. I shall argue in chapters 4 and 5 that foster-parents need the offer of 'casework help': this is not a conventional view, neither is it realistic or even ethical in terms of some definitions of casework, but in my present terms (of its being a way of helping people to get on with each other) it seems shiningly clear that anybody bound up with troubled children, including the children who test the binding, may need to express their feelings about it to someone outside the immediate circle, in order that they may live more harmoniously together. (Lest this sound as though the caseworker is a universal remedy, it is worth remembering that he too needs support and supervision.) Much child care and family casework consists in making plans and putting these into operation for varying periods, and it seems essential to regard the plans in relation to the thoughts and feelings of those concerned. Of course it would be invasion of privacy to diagnose and treat a caretaker as though he or she were a client who has requested this kind of help, but emotional problems do arise for almost any adult entrusted with someone else's child, and part of the service should allow for discussion of relationship difficulties.

An attempt was made in chapter 2 to draw some distinction between caseworker and psychotherapist, seeing the latter as a subjective figure in the child's eyes and the former concerned with external events and people in the child's life as well as with the child's feelings about them. This implies that the caseworker tends not so much to explore the past within the current transference situation as to focus on current events and to take direct action in them. The action required is sometimes drastic, causing children to regard their workers as extraordinarily powerful people, which in turn gives opportunity for them to experience that authority-figures can be considerate and friendly. Holman (1966) showed that many of his small sample of children in care saw their caseworkers as acceptable home-finders rather than as body-snatchers. Caseworkers sometimes have difficulty in knowing when to refer children for psychiatric help, and it is tempting not only to refer those who appear disturbed by intra-psychic conflicts but also those who are in fact reacting quite healthily to current upheavals, and to attempt to transfer the whole worrying situation into the lap of the psychiatric team in the expectation of a miracle. The team's function may be to give background support to the caseworker who continues to persevere in the foreground.

Psychiatric help is even less available to many families than is a casework service. C. Winnicott (1964, pp. 41-9) clarifies the difference between the two, partly in emphasising the caseworker's strength as an ordinary person conveying willingness to try to understand communications. Dockar Drysdale (1968, p. 29) in a similar way distinguishes between *interpretation*, which implies a translation of the unconscious content of speech or action into a conscious form available for consideration by the patient and the therapist, and *communication*, in which the worker responds with some regard to deeper meaning but in the terms presented to him. I suggest that ability to communicate thus is within the scope of casework and that it is necessary in each case to be open (in a sensitive, discriminating manner) to the possibility of communicating with anybody involved in it, perhaps focusing on different members according to their apparent needs and what *other sources of help are available* at any particular stage. Although there is great value in direct casework with children, I consider it even more important to help parent-figures to help the children with whom they are actually living.

4

Children in special circumstances

There may be intelligence or sparks of the divinity in millions—but they are not souls until they acquire identity, till each one is personally itself ... As various as the Lives of Men are—so various become their Souls ... and what was [man's] Soul before it came into the world ...? An intelligence—without Identity—and how is this Identity to be made? Through the medium of the heart? and how is the Heart to become this Medium but in a world of Circumstances?

(from *The Letters of John Keats*)

I have an odd way of sometimes, as it were, being able to see myself through someone else's eyes. Then I view the affairs of a certain 'Anne' at my ease; and browse through the pages of her life as if she were a stranger. Before we came here, when I didn't think about things as much as I do now, I used at times to have the feeling that I didn't belong ... Sometimes I used to pretend I was an orphan, until I reproached myself ...

(*The Diary of Anne Frank*, aged 15)

Infants becoming a charge on the parish ... were to be baptised within 14 days and their name and sur-name to be entered into the register 'and in case of a difficulty of distinguishing children, some proper mark shall be affixed to the child's cloathes, or hung round his or her neck.'

(from an Act of 1762, quoted by Pinchbeck and Hewitt)

This chapter introduces, in a compressed form, work with children in a variety of special circumstances: it draws attention to some of the relevant study and research and explores some of the crucial ideas. There is value in attempting occasionally to prune back to essentials, because experienced workers can become so accustomed to peculiar circumstances that they risk either a lack of clarity in viewing the over-all pattern of the wood or a blunting of their imaginative response to individual trees, whereas new workers may become entangled in a forest of live and dead vegetation. Research (e.g. George, 1970; Triseliotis, 1970) reveals a disquieting gap between what we believe in theory and what we do in practice. Possibly the gap exists partly because the theory itself is undeveloped and the task is crisis-ridden, with workers constantly facing difficult decisions while supported by limited resources.

Several themes could be traced throughout the chapter, and three of these are selected for preliminary consideration:

1. the relevance of crisis-theory to the difficulty found by those involved in visualising most of these situations in advance, and in living them through;
2. the practical relevance of the physical development of the children;
3. the importance of the self-image of all these children, and the difficulty that many experience in acquiring a clear sense of identity.

Crisis-intervention, grief and mourning

People caught up in a current crisis are thought by crisis-theorists (e.g. Caplan, 1961; Parad, 1965) to be particularly susceptible to social work help, which may offer a chance for them to correct previous maladaptive problem-solving and especially to discover effective ways of meeting possible future upheavals. Caplan's simplest definition of crisis is 'an upset in a steady state'; others term it 'any sharp or decisive change for which old patterns are inadequate'. Hill (1965) classifies family troubles partly by their effect upon family configuration: *dismemberment* (loss of a member or role); *accession* (addition of an unprepared-for member or role) and *demoralisation* (loss of morale and family unity). Some family crises involve two or even three of these aspects: e.g. adoption, fostering, desertion, handicap.

Types of crisis can be seen *either* as maturational/developmental—stages of normal life from birth to death; Parad contains papers on various stages, often in terms of role-transition; *or* as situational/accidental—e.g. a railway disaster affecting many people, or loss of job affecting a man and his dependents. One merciful characteristic of the theoretical state of crisis is that it does not continue indefinitely. Even though it brings painful feelings of tension, helplessness and confusion, it has certain typical phases during which some solution (hopefully a constructive one) is found. Lindemann (1965) observed such phases in his research into the symptoms and management of acute grief (see Bowlby, 1960; also Rutter, 1966, has two chapters on bereavement in childhood). Grief results not only from bereavement by death, but in many situations involving loss, separation and deprivation—e.g. surgery, handicap, eviction, imprisonment, reception into care, childlessness, divorce; loss of job, status or role. Briefly, grief symptoms are bodily distress (sighing, emptiness, exhaustion), preoccupation with the lost object, guilt, hostility, and loss of customary patterns of behaviour.

'Grief work' (Caplan, 1961, pp. 58-62) is seen as a necessary, though painful, process towards recovery; a person may need support in accepting this process of acknowledging the loss, reviewing the past, expressing guilt and hostility, and beginning to meet a new future. Unhealthy grief reactions may include escape into over-activity, psychosomatic illness, unexpressed hostility causing wooden behaviour, continuing lack of concentration and purpose, deterioration in relationships ... Sometimes delayed reaction to an earlier bereavement is precipitated by a further loss. The treatment of morbid grief towards 'normal grief' requires a willingness to help the person to undertake his grief work. Such work is relevant to many of the children and adults who appear throughout this chapter. 'Worry work' (Caplan, pp. 43-58) is parallel to grief work: a means of preparing for a possible crisis by anticipating it emotionally beforehand. Moderate worry work, such as preparing a child for hospital or foster-care, alleviates subsequent distress. But there is some danger of doing the anticipatory work too thoroughly when the dreaded event does not happen—e.g. a mother may not feel quite the same towards her new baby if she was first prepared for his possible death or handicap and subsequently told he is healthy after all.

There is some link between the maturational aspects of crisis (and the way people involved in crisis-situations perceive their problem) and my second theme:

The practical relevance of physical development

Children vary in size from being as transportable as a parcel to surpassing the worker's own stature. Research (Parker, 1966; George, 1970) shows that the younger the child, the more likely he is to adapt to a new, permanent home—perhaps babies are almost too convenient to move, considering the long-term implications of hastily planning their lives. Babies cannot choose where they go, but it seems they are keenly aware of the unfamiliar feel of new parent-figures (and equipment). A baby's distress is sometimes intense when he is first introduced to prospective adopters, and it can be pathetic to see the latter's attempts to make him smile at them, when the mutual tension might be reduced if he were held quietly with his face turned inwards to the new mother-figure's shoulder.

In contrast, a truculent adolescent sometimes seems impossible to shift except by force; the resistant body may be heavily mature though its emotions are those of a fearful, defiant toddler. It happens more often in residential work than in field work that verbal encouragement proves futile, and the combined strength of two or more adults seems regrettably to be the only method of locomotion. An effective alternative to physical force is to offer the defiant adolescent one's hand or arm, perhaps saying, 'Take my hand and come with me'—the toddler in them responds almost involuntarily without further fight or flight. The worker should not make the complete gesture of taking hold of the adolescent as this would probably precipitate a struggle, but should offer her own hand within a few inches so that the other person can choose to respond in a small way.

A further practical consideration is the vulnerability of male workers to the possible sexual allegations of adolescent girls: probably the only protection necessary is awareness of the fantasies easily sparked off in emotionally-starved girls, and the mixture of spontaneous discretion required in any professional relationship, with an occasional thought as to the advisability of having a third person present in potentially inflammable situations like long car-journeys. There is also the question of how best to protect children suffering from sexual assault by disturbed, immature men. First, it seems that a child is often a party to the offence—i.e. deprived children tend to be attention-seeking, intrigued by overtures showing interest, easily bribed with sweets and money (see Burton, 1968). Secondly, it is thought that the aftermath of questioning and the shocked or punitive reactions of parent figures can be far more damaging than the event itself; the main impression on the child centres in the kindness or otherwise of responsible adults concerned. Incest is a much more complex situation, but again its effect on the young person is probably determined largely by the repercussions on family relationships.

Kirk (1964) stresses the need for adopted children to discuss their situation progressively, alongside their understanding of human relationships. Similarly, children in care (e.g. Hitchman, 1960) feel their circumstances differently at successive stages, and it may be particularly difficult for them to account for themselves at new schools or in employment and courtship. Handicapped children tend to become less acceptable in the community once sexually mature. The mother of a severely handicapped child may have to tend him indefinitely as though he were a baby; this not only becomes more incongruous with bodily-growth, but an increasing tax on her sheer physical strength as she simultaneously ages. A particularly relevant example is the battered child, typically under three years old. (Older children have some protection in being able to speak of ill-treatment and of being observed at school.) An observed feature of 'battering parents' is their misperception of the child's true identity. It almost seems as though the battered baby's best hope of self-protection lies in his acquiring the three-year-old's sense of identity, though this achievement is not encouraged by parental ambivalence. The third theme follows naturally:

Self-image, and difficulties in acquiring a sense of identity

Questions such as 'Who am I?', 'Where do I belong?', 'Where am I going?' cannot always be answered clearly in a static moment, though they are more urgent and therefore sometimes grasped in moments of stress: usually a person has an indefinable, developing sense of identity over the years of changing external circumstances. Some relevant writers are Erikson, Argyle, Lynd, Laing (who must be left to speak for himself—e.g. 1961, chapter 7), Goffman, Escalona and Coopersmith. Argyle (1967, extended in 1969) says that self-image, or ego-identity, is concerned with how a person perceives himself; self-esteem refers to self-evaluation—how favourably he regards himself. (Clearly the two are closely related, as there is no incentive to picture oneself unless something pleasant can be seen.) He outlines the origins of the self-image: first, the *reactions* of other people—'to see ourselves, we look to see how we are reflected in the reactions of others'; secondly, the *comparison* of self with others who are 'constantly present and sufficiently similar to invite comparison'; thirdly, the *roles* a person plays at various stages. A child plays at many parts before needing to commit himself; adolescents tend to choose through experimentation which part to emphasise (see Erikson, 1968; Nursten, 1964).

Many children, typically in pre-adolescence, write down their address in relation to the whole world and beyond: 'Linda Kay, 24 Oak Close, Nortown, Yorkshire, England, Europe, The World, The Universe'. A central core of the self-image is a person's name, body-image, sex, age, occupation, plus factors such as religion, social class, special achievements or anything that marks him out as different from others. It is comfortable to fit into a natural group; otherwise a person feels isolated; he belongs nowhere and has no norms for guidance. Argyle suggests that roles provide an easy solution to the problem of ego-identity—but can be burdensome, since so much of the self cannot be fitted into a particular role. Ruddock (1969) questions whether personality can fully be described in role terms. Perlman (1966) discusses the malaise resulting from an impaired sense of identity, which may undermine capacity for work and relationships. She suggests that clients commonly present identity problems in terms of their difficulty in fulfilling social roles, so can be helped by the caseworker focusing on the current role. 'A socially recognised role is a kind of anchorage; it links a person to at least one other, giving a sense of belonging; the function expressed by the role gives purpose.'

The child's view of his sameness or difference is clearly important: Goffman and Scheff use a sociological approach to these ideas. Goffman (1963) describes how the person with a stigma is marked in some way as different, with all the disgrace this implies. He distinguishes between the plight of the *discredited* person whose stigma is evident at first sight (e.g. a thalidomide child) and the position of the *discreditable* person whose stigma is not immediately apparent but discoverable by others (e.g. a foster-child). He lists three types of stigma: the various physical deformities; blemishes of character inferable from a person's record, and the tribal stigma of race, nation and religion. (Some people in this chapter are stigmatised in all three ways.) He goes on to describe the uneasiness, at least initially, of social interaction between a stigmatised and a 'normal' person. Two sympathetic, though still ambiguous, groups are available to the former: those of his own kind, and those who make themselves 'wise' to his condition through partial identification—social workers presumably are wise in this way, and so are regarded ambivalently both by the marked person and by society. Scheff (1966) studies the persistent need of 'normal' people to label others apparently suffering mental illness, and to force them into behaviour deemed appropriate to the label.

Coopersmith's research (1967) attempted to clarify the antecedents of self-esteem: these he summarised briefly as *parental warmth, clearly defined limits* and *respectful treatment*. There seems to be a general relationship between parents' self-esteem and the manner in which they treat their children. His findings suggest strongly that children with high self-esteem are less likely to display anxiety and are better able to meet threats to security when these do arise. The families of children with high self-esteem had well-defined limits of behaviour co-existing with greater tolerance for individual expression and less drastic forms of punishment; families producing creative and assertive children are those which accept and respect their children. 'Persons with low self-esteem, reared under conditions of rejection, uncertainty and disrespect, have come to believe they are powerless and without resource or recourse. They feel isolated, unlovable, incapable of expressing and defending themselves' (see also Farber, 1970).

Erikson (1950, 1968) and Lynd (1958) are particularly useful in exploring ideas about the search for identity. Erikson's 'Eight ages of man' (1950, ch. 7) traces the development of ego-identity, beginning with the baby's first social achievement: his willingness to let his mother out of sight without undue anxiety and rage 'because she has become an inner certainty as well as an outer predictability'. (Perhaps the grief work mentioned above is not only a process of shedding the past but also of gradually replacing the external loss with a comforting internal image.) Escalona's tome (1969) studies in minute detail 'the roots of individuality' which develop in babies during the first six months of life. Erikson summarises his ideas thus: 'The sense of ego-identity, then, is the accrued confidence that one's ability to maintain inner sameness and continuity ... is matched by the sameness and continuity of one's meaning for others.' His later work (1968) is specifically about youth, identity and crisis—an extension of former ideas. Lynd (1958) draws upon English literature, philosophy, sociology, psychology, in order to look at the nature of shame and its possible use in the search for identity. She distinguishes between feelings of guilt (arising from a sense of wrong-doing) and the deeper feelings of shame which arise from a sense of inferiority.

Characteristic of shame, Lynd says, is the sudden exposure of unexpected incongruity, the apparently trivial incident which arouses excessively painful emotion, the threat to the core of identity; the loss of trust in expectations of oneself, of other persons, of one's society, and a reluctant questioning of meaning in the world—all these things combine to make experiences of shame almost impossible to communicate. She describes the acute conflict felt by children (e.g. of immigrant families) caught between the desire to look up to their parents and the shame felt through exposure of parental weakness and differentness. Also, 'just as shame for one's parents in some ways tests the limits of one's acceptance of oneself, so shame for and with one's children comes near to testing the limits of one's faith in the possibilities of life.' Lynd then moves on to discuss whether the *self-revealing* (and world-revealing) nature of experiences of shame might offer a clue to the discovery of identity. She sees two possibilities: first, that experiences of shame may lead to protection of the exposed self and of the exposed society at all costs, resulting in refusal to recognise the wound, depersonalisation and superficiality. Or secondly, if it is possible to face experiences of shame, 'they may throw light on who one is, and hence point the way toward who and what one may become.' I would add that people suffering shame frequently require support and acceptance if they are to find courage to face it; also it can be painful for caretakers and fieldworkers to empathise with people in special circumstances.

These somewhat lengthy preliminaries should, if they can be kept in mind, enable brevity throughout the rest of the chapter.

Single-parent families

Young (1954), Wimperis (1960), Pochin (1969) consider unmarried mothers and their needs; Wynn (1964, 1970) and Marsden (1969) study the difficulties experienced by fatherless families; also some writers on adoption (Rowe, 1966, Goodacre, 1966) include useful sections on unmarried parents. I recommend Holman's concise, well-documented study (1970) on unsupported mothers and the care of their children. Members of the pressure group 'Mothers in Action' were both the subjects of Holman's survey and the publishers of his report. These ninety-five mothers included two divorcees and two women separated from their husbands. They were of a higher socio-economic group than many others in similar circumstances, yet they experienced prolonged poverty of living, frustration and anxiety in their efforts to care for their children—all of which implies even greater suffering amongst less 'fortunate' groups. Holman found that many mothers had great difficulty in securing adequate income, accommodation and day care. 'The reasons for their difficulties are no doubt multiple but are related to the availability of support from their kin, the provisions made by the social services, the personal capacities of the mothers, and the attitudes of society as a whole.' Both the mothers and their children were at risk of social and emotional deprivation, especially in the first two years; the greatest risk is separation from each other.

Mothers in Action themselves are sympathetic towards the plight of unsupported *fathers* caring for children. Such men, who may be bereaved or deserted, sometimes make heavy weather of housekeeping; they too have the strain of carrying a double role, and some feel unable to express grief about the loss of their partner. The children may not be allowed to speak of their lost mother if the father fears crying in front of the children or remains bitter about her departure. It is a lonely life for either a father or a mother; a social worker can sometimes take part in the kind of discussion (e.g. of the children's progress) which a married couple might normally enjoy together. The situation can be eased a little with community support and comprehensive social services. An unsupported, expectant mother cannot make a proper decision about the future if her choice lies merely between struggling alone or giving up the child for adoption. The 'permissive' society may have resulted in fewer babies being available for adoption, but this unfortunately is not because the burden on single parents has been lightened appreciably. Many girls start off hopefully but become disheartened over a lengthy period.

The unsupported mother is liable to over-invest in her baby as one person who will love her selflessly. She may manage initially through her own mother's willingness to look after the baby while she goes out to work, but the child may gradually become torn between two possessive mother-figures. Children in single-parent families are vulnerable, and liable to become confused about family relationships. There is growing recognition that adoption should not be used to confuse or distort existing relationships— e.g. it is unnecessary for a mother to adopt her own child or for grandparents to turn into legal parents. This section dovetails with the next; most of the following sections overlap.

Adoption

First, I would like to consider the essence of adoption.

Suppose there are two stages in 'having a baby':
initially, the obvious stage of conception, pregnancy
and confinement; secondly, from birth onwards, the
prolonged giving of daily care while the child is
dependent upon grown-ups. Whether or not maternal

feelings arise spontaneously with the baby's birth, out of the very activity of subsequent daily caring inevitably grows some real feeling of a parent-child relationship. In adoption these two stages are split. The 'natural' mother is always the one who gave birth, but she cannot feel a complete mother without living through the second stage. The adoptive parents miss the first stage, but hope to experience as much as possible of the second. The prolonged giving of daily care confers parenthood on adopters—the Court Order is confirmation of a genuine human experience. The original parent is often called the 'real', 'natural' or 'biological' parent, but surely changing nappies, frequent feeding and bringing up wind is equally real—so perhaps both stages include some physical relationship and a large emotional content. Both women naturally grieve over the fact that they each give only one stage instead of the normal and essential two. In this they have something in common, however different they may appear superficially. They mourn separately but come together in the developing child. As it is the adoptive parents who will be providing long-term care, it becomes their responsibility to try to hold the two stages together for the child, so that he may grow up with a sense of continuity and self-esteem from the beginning.

The above accords with current thinking about adoption, practised throughout civilisation, though ideas about its nature and purpose develop and become crystallised in law, in recent years with considerable rapidity. An A C C O monograph (1969) and the working paper of the Houghton Committee (H M S O, 1970) reflect the quality of imaginative thought given nowadays to issues surrounding adoption. The welfare of the child himself is now established as the foremost consideration, with the most controversial question centring on how best to reconcile this with the natural mother's right to have a reasonable length of time in which to decide on her baby's future. Recent thinking is concerned particularly with helping adoptive parents to

bring up their child from the beginning in a positive knowledge of his circumstances.

Though it was generally accepted earlier that it is essential to tell the child the plain fact of his adoption (if
merely as a precaution against his eventual rebellious dis-
illusionment), we are becoming more aware of the subtle-
ties inherent in such telling. Adopters may readily agree
in theory beforehand, but find it difficult 'to tell' in subsequent practice because of the personal implications of
infertility and illegitimacy. It is unhelpful if they convey
to the child that he was originally unwanted but later
highly desirable to them, as this suggests initial rejection
solved by importunate baby-snatchers. Once it was thought
encouraging to tell adopted children that they were
specially chosen—now we realise that being 'chosen' risks
the child later feeling inadequate in meeting the expectations determining his earlier selection. Again, it was once
deemed unnecessary for adopters to know anything about
the original parents; then followed a swing towards complete candour in sharing information; now (see Rowe,
1966, pp. 220-3) it is thought best to give a full picture
whilst withholding details (e.g. that this is a woman's
fourth illegitimate child) which are irrelevant in terms
of heredity but which may prove burdensome.

These ideas have been stimulated by Kirk (1964), himself
an adopter, whose research theme is that adoption is a
real but different way of creating a family; if it is to bring
fulfilment, the adoptive parents should acknowledge rather
than 'deny the difference': thus they may help their child
to accept his circumstances, and integrate themselves as a
developing family. (Humphrey, 1969, pp. 78-80, does not
find Kirk's evidence wholly convincing, nor perhaps intellectually digestible to simple folk. Again, to some people,
adoption seems an over-convenient means of evading issues
surrounding the plight of natural parents.) Corollaries to
Kirk's central idea of the 'shared fate' of the child and his

85

two sets of parents are as follows:

1. Prospective adopters may be partially self-selecting (assuming they satisfy certain basic criteria of health, age and marital status) through education to a point where they can decide whether this form of parenthood is appropriate for them personally.
2. A worker's attempts to 'match' child and adopters in terms of physical and intellectual factors are less relevant if the child is not going to be regarded as their own conception. But adopters need to know about themselves, about the child and his first parents, in order to make a successful graft. There is room for less secrecy when differences implicit in adoption are acknowledged both in society and in a specific family.
3. The child grows up in a progressive knowledge of his circumstances, and relates this to his understanding of family relationships as it develops. The developmental approach means that adoptive families may welcome casework help or group discussion at various stages from babyhood up through adolescence.

The details of the child's story matter both in their origin and in their subsequent telling: therefore the social worker has a responsibility both for helping adopters to consider ways of communicating the story and for her own actions within the story itself—i.e. the history is less acceptable to the child later if it contains disparaging facts such as, 'You were handed over to us in a car park ... the court hearing was over so quickly it didn't seem true'. (To many, the court appearance does come as an anti-climax, and some adopters may like to know of the Board of Social Responsibility's 'Service of Blessing for an Adopted Child'.) Kirk (1964, chapter 10) suggests the need for sensitive response to the child's indirect requests for information and support—direct questions may never be asked if the child senses they cause tension. A child cannot easily comprehend how 'love' could have motivated his first mother to relinquish him; he only gradually visualises the problems of an unsupported mother. Non-verbal communication may include a toy, photograph or item of clothing provided by the first mother; a celebration of the adoption anniversary or a tree-planting ceremony. Sharrar (1970) suggests singing a home-made song or writing a simple story for subsequent use when placing older babies.

Relevant literature includes Rowe (1959, 1966); Goodacre (1966) who includes a consumer viewpoint of ninety adoptive families in their first few years' experience; Pugh (1968, chapter 7); and McWhinnie (1967, abbreviated in 1969) who studied the life histories of fifty-eight adults adopted in early childhood, including six near-'adopted' foster-children. Her finding—that adolescents identify primarily with their adoptive parents—is reassuring, but almost all these fifty-eight adults had wanted factual information about their original parents. They were both curious and apprehensive of what they might find out, and felt rootless in knowing little or nothing. Boys may have extra need to know something of their putative fathers, of whom little may be known by anyone. There is a comprehensive guide to adoption practice (H M S O, 1970); Pringle (1967) reviews research material; D. Winnicott (1957, chapter 8) describes the development of two adopted siblings into adulthood; and Tod's collected papers (1971 a) survey casework and group work practice.

Recent developments include study and emphasis on the possibility of placing handicapped/older/coloured children for adoption, and of the agency's responsibility to offer follow-up services for adoptive families. Raynor (1970) reports on a project which studied adoption across racial lines; a main conclusion was that suitable homes can be found, though of course each child requires individual consideration. Kadushin (1970) found a high success rate in his follow-up study of older children selected as suitable for adoption, having earlier been removed from neglectful or abusive natural parents; he thinks we underestimate children's ability to outgrow destructive experience once they are settled into a benign environment. Andrews (1971) debates whether financially subsidised adoption, for reasons of the children's race, health or age, is sometimes preferable to long-term foster-care. Lawder (1970) and contributors to Tod's collection (1971 a) advocate the availability of post-adoptive counselling. Workers may overlook emotional problems at the time of placement through colluding with the 'happiness aura' surrounding new adopters; subsequent meetings enable a thread of continuity for the child, and may be directed towards modifying harsh parental expectations. Rowe and Kornitzer (1968), studying breakdown in the early stages of adoption placements, show that second placements to couples who have previously adopted a child are not without hazard.

Linking this section with the next, Rowe (1971) contrasts reality and fantasy elements impinging on the foster-child and on the adopted child; she concludes that the latter is in a relatively strong position.

Foster-care

In so far as one can discuss foster-care other than in terms of triangular relationships, the children themselves are considered in this section; their parents and caretakers appear in chapter 5. Mapstone (1971, p. 98) conveys a glimpse of the underlying fantasies in all parties which may heighten the realistic tensions in this complex, delicate web of relationships:

The natural mother and the foster-mother ... if there are two mothers then there is an accepted tradition running from the judgment of Solomon, through legend and fairy-tales to the television documentaries of the present day: a tradition which maintains that one mother must be good and one must be bad ... The baby in his own home comes to the knowledge that the two mothers are one, but in foster care there are in reality two separate people and between them stand the child and the social worker.

Mapstone, *née* Pugh (1968, chapter 5) provides a concise description of foster-care.

It is important first to appreciate that short-term foster-care, especially for young children, is as serious in its implications as long-term care (though uncertainties for all concerned may be greatest during a highly unpredictable 'middle-term' period—as Parker (1966) points out, much can be borne if a time limit is foreseen). Schaffer and Schaffer (1968) studied 100 families whose children were received briefly into care during the mother's confinement in hospital, comparing these with a control group which made private arrangements. Families in the former group were found to be more isolated both from relatives (geographically and emotionally) and within the community, more dependent on public services; with the fathers participating less in family life, and the mothers (many of whom had suffered early deprivation) apparently less involved with their young children, who had more frequently experienced previous separation in care or in hospital. Pre-school children were most vulnerable to being sent away because of their 'nuisance value' in needing constant attention. The Schaffers conclude that short-term care matters not only in terms of emotional suffering but because it is so often a symptom of a general inadequacy in the family. To treat automatically such an application for care is to 'neglect the appeal for help and to go counter to the currently advocated spirit of prevention'.

The Schaffers had the impression that some local authorities were almost too accommodating in providing short-term care on request; they quote Fitzherbert's finding (1967) that, when workers were firm in refusing to consider reception of West Indian children into care except as a last resort, forgotten relatives and previously unwilling fathers suddenly appeared and took charge. While it may be true that some immigrant parents perceive foster-care as providing 'a good English upbringing', I question the validity of Fitzherbert's recommendation which, according to Holman (ed. 1970, p. 203) has resulted sometimes in discrimination against immigrant families in real need. Clearly, every application for care requires careful thought and discussion with the family before a joint decision can be reached, and the worker has a responsibility for helping the family seek suitable alternative plans where possible— e.g. private (paid) fostering with relatives/neighbours, arrangements involving the father's employment, the use of day nurseries and home helps. A short period of good care can sometimes form part of a long-term plan in preventive casework—e.g. when a mother is temporarily ill or overwhelmed.

Workers try to visualise the possible effects of alternative plans, in relation to the facilities available to the department. (There is insufficient space here to consider privately-arranged foster-care, but recent changes in child protection law enable more positive, flexible statutory oversight of such children, of whom young coloured children probably constitute a particularly vulnerable group. Again, foster-care by close relatives cannot be discussed fully here; such an arrangement has advantages in theory—in practice much depends on the balance of strong ambivalence likely to be shown between related parent-figures.) Jehu's monograph (1963) explores factors affecting the worker's decision to receive and support a child into care. Stevenson (1968) discusses the emotional meaning of reception into care for all concerned. Kadushin (1967, via George, 1970) summarises the child's likely feelings in separation:

feelings of rejection which engender feelings of worthlessness; guilt which may lead the child to feel he has contributed to breaking up the home; hostility which reinforces the guilt, because hostile feelings—particularly against one's own parents—are a punishable offence; fear of abandonment, fear of the unknown; shame.

Anything which can be done to ease the child's feelings and to prepare him (as well as his adults) for the fostering experience, vitally affects its outcome. Indeed, much can be done, though at least three factors affect the worker's ability to help: pressures of work in making even the barest practical plans; pressures from well-meaning adults who try to ignore the pain, and the worker's own belief that separation is so damaging and foster-care so risky that little can be done except plan it superficially in a spirit of fatalism. It requires courage for the worker to let himself appear to precipitate negative reactions from the child for the sake of long-term emotional gains—it is certainly tidier to deliver a numb child to a foster-home, to slip away without saying goodbye and to agree that subsequent parental visiting will only upset him. However, the child needs to discuss at each stage what is happening, why care is necessary, how long it may last and to see where siblings are living. It makes all the difference to have an introductory visit to the foster-home, preferably with a parent or well-known adult who will also accompany him with the worker on the day of reception (so he knows that his family knows where he is), and if future visits can be discussed beforehand. Children are remarkably resilient and adaptable when given a chance. Verbal communication often has to be repetitious, reinforced in non-verbal ways—a photograph of his parent(s), some of his own toys and possessions, postcards, maps, calendar —according to age and inclination (see Lomax-Simpson 1964, 1966).

These communications continue to be important while the child remains in care. Records should include brief, pleasantly-evocative, human details of the child's relatives and home, as well as plain facts. Introductions to a long-term foster-home should be extended over a flexible period according to the child's apparent readiness for the final move—closely-spaced visits for a young child; time to assimilate events for an older child. Charnley (1955) and Glickman (1957) are helpful on these aspects. It is easier for the child to meet prospective foster-parents first in his accustomed surroundings. He needs to know what to call them ('Auntie and Uncle' seem somewhat over-used by deprived children) and they should use his own name rather than change it to their preference. Sants (1964) discusses the 'genealogical bewilderment' of children with substitute parents, which presumably is caused partly through acquiring artificial branches to the original family tree, though Sants relates it usefully to the story of 'The Ugly Duckling'. Weinstein (1960) studied the self-image of foster-children and found greater well-being amongst those whose natural parents visited them regularly, whether or not they identified primarily with their foster-parents.

One method of enhancing a child's sense of identity, especially when he has known numerous changes of address, is to compile an illustrated story/photograph album of his life history. This may cost about £3 to complete; it can be done with the child's help, whilst being presented as attractively as possible. It means extracting a story from a bulky file (though ideally the album is started at the time of reception into care), editing the story in its true, human but best light (with subsequent discussion of more painful aspects) and illustrating it with photographs of relevant people and places, postcards of places, magazine pictures ... Some foster-children lead extremely dislocated lives so that in late-adolescence and courtship they can only explain themselves lamely—'I was a foster-child'. It also helps other people's opinion of them if they can convey a coherent life-story with something good in it. Parent-figures often become enthusiastic in helping to compile the book. The agency can keep a stock of frequently-used photographs e.g. of the Reception Centre. If the worker has insufficient time for such frills, the compilation can be a mutually useful exercise for a student during a field-work placement.

Students are sometimes excluded from long-term fostering situations but can offer a valuable contribution of concentrated attention to some aspect of it—perhaps in tracing natural parents, drawing out the foster-father, listening to the foster-mother's account of her vicissitudes, taking the child to re-visit old haunts. This raises the question of the worker's relationship with foster-parents—to which I will return later; meanwhile Thomas (1971) expands the idea of helping foster-parents to understand disturbed children in order to counteract previous unsatisfactory experiences. Often foster-parents are given only stark background information—'mother deserted while father in prison'—and are left feeling critical and uneasy. These details need discussion in terms of their actual effects on the child and current ways of helping him as a whole person. Foster-parents gain confidence through the joint planning of constructive future measures, having gained some imaginative understanding of the past. Enlightening papers about understanding and helping variously-disturbed children are those of C. Winnicott (1968, pp. 73-9) and Woodmansey (1966 b). Stevenson (1965), in writing directly to foster-parents of young children, shows how we may convey crucial ideas in simple, practical words.

It is difficult to evaluate research studies on foster-care : this is partly because the number of large-scale longitudinal studies is limited—some are American and therefore not wholly applicable; even within Britain there are wide regional variations in child care policy and practice (see Packman, 1968); also it is not easy to find appropriate control groups, nor to isolate factors in situations of such complexity, and some findings become less relevant with rapid developments in the child care service since 1948. Inevitably therefore, studies do not validate each other consistently; they tend fruitfully to raise more questions than they answer, so it may be best here to comment broadly, making limited mention of detailed findings immediately relevant in practice. I recommend scrutiny of a combination of Dinnage and Pringle's review of research (1967 a) with a more recent study by George (1970).

Classic pieces of research are those of Parker (1966) and Trasler (1960). Parker found a success rate—defined as five years' unbroken foster-care—of 52 per cent in 209 long-term placements. His main confirmations were that the child's age is crucial ('as far as fostering is concerned—the younger the better'); the presence of children of the family about the age of the foster-child is a situation likely to produce difficulty; children with behaviour disturbances are difficult to foster—though not necessarily those with physical handicaps. Parker's results largely confirmed those of Trasler, who emphasised the importance of the child's social environment both before and after the event of separation—also the painful effects of breakdown on foster-parents themselves.

George (1970) is essential reading, with useful evaluation of former study in relation to his own, pointing out discrepancies between theory and practice. His failure rate was 59·8 per cent of 128 long-term placements with non-related foster-parents within a period of five years. His study confirmed that the risk of breakdown is very high during the first two years of placement, which implies the need for workers to give concentrated support then. In his exploration as to whether outcome is related to specific factors, it appeared that foster-children who had previously spent a short period in residential care were more successful (possibly because placements from there could be made more carefully); that foster-mothers aged

under forty but over twenty-five years were more successful (Trasler and Parker found those over forty rather more
successful); that the quality of the natural home is positively related to outcome; that the placement of two or
more siblings in the same home requires great care. It
looked as though, when workers were aware of potential
difficulties because of former research findings (e.g. near-
ness in age of the foster-parents' own child), more care was
taken to deal with the risks involved and therefore these
placements were more successful. This is perhaps the
main practical value of research—awareness of risk enables
workers to allocate time and effort accordingly.

On the whole George found little difference between
trained and untrained workers—practice seemed to be influenced more by over-all policy in the three departments
than by individual approach. Initial assessment reports on
prospective foster-parents contained vague phrases instead
of 'portraying real people with strengths and weaknesses';
workers lacked criteria for the assessment of marital relationships and child-rearing attitudes when selecting foster-
parents; matching of child and foster-home was somewhat
sketchy; foster-fathers were neglected. There was confusion
between workers and foster-parents about their relationship
(the term 'colleague' proved fairly meaningless on both
sides) and uncertainty about the role-content of foster-
parenthood. George thinks the name 'foster-parent' might
be changed to 'foster-care worker', whose main satisfaction
would lie in doing a job well, and in being paid for it.
(Adamson, 1969, pleads for better treatment of foster-
parents.) In all, George's study showed a need for greater
administrative support of fieldworkers, for better planning
in recruiting, selecting and maintaining foster-homes, and
in caring for natural parents.

More knowledge is needed about what makes fostering
succeed from the child's point of view. Ferguson (1966)
provides one example of a study of young adults who had

been in care—in many cases subsequent relationships with foster-parents were good and contact was maintained. R. Jenkins (1965) examined the adjustment between foster-parents and children in ninety-seven current foster-homes, and concluded that in sixty-seven cases relationships were satisfactory in that the foster-parents were finding some emotional fulfilment. Jenkins later (1969) suggests that, if the needs of foster-parents have been accurately assessed, long-term fostering is likely to meet the child's needs if the child is under eighteen months old at placement and/or if regular contact with the natural family can be maintained. Motivations for fostering can be extremely complex —akin to icebergs not in temperature but in the proportion which is overt. Initially workers focus on the applicants' own interest, hopes and fears about fostering, rather than visit with a particular child in mind. It is hard for people to visualise what fostering will actually entail—one couple said reproachfully, when reviewing their first year's experience, 'We didn't know about the emotional side'. Applicants may gain insight through direct discussion with an experienced foster-parent. Fortunately foster-parents are assumed to have personal, though one hopes not overwhelming, needs nowadays—the worker's skill lies in assessing these, visualising them in relation to a particular child, and in being supportive throughout (see Kay, 1966, 1967). The children are so diverse in age and in situational requirements that suitable foster-parents can also range widely in their particular circumstances.

Probably there would be fewer crises and breakdowns if foster-parents had sufficient confidence in themselves and in their workers to admit difficulties at an early stage. Timms (1962), in two very helpful chapters on working with foster-parents, suggests that foster-care breakdowns are basically connected with *breakdown in the relationship between worker and foster-parent*. Tod's collected papers (1971 b) contain encouraging contributions on casework and group work with all parties in the fostering triangle—especially valuable is Stanley on the group method of educating and selecting foster-parents, Kay on selecting and conserving these precious resources, accounts of group discussions with foster-children, and a letter from an adolescent girl in care to her grandmother:

> I wondered if you were in a position to tell me a few details of my origin ... I am fifteen years old and one month and in a position to be told more than I have been ... If my mother couldn't possibly have kept me, then tell me why ... Once I know I can settle down with [my foster-parents] with an easy heart, not one that wonders all the time ...

The whole letter should be read and re-read.

Finally there are the children who drift on in care, perhaps with many changes of home or in poor placements which workers dare not terminate. Such drifting is as serious a problem as legal fighting between parents and foster-parents for possession of the child—mentioned below in chapter 5. Maas and Engler (1959) predicted, on the basis of frequency of parental visiting combined with evidence of future plans, that at least half a very large group of children would spend the major part of their childhood away from home. Ten years later (1969) Maas found his prediction largely true, and that the remaining children seemed most deprived in their relationships and abilities. Fanshel (1971) gives an interim report on a five-year longitudinal study of 624 children who entered foster-care in New York City for the first time in their lives in 1966. The major exodus out of care occurred during the first year when thirty per cent of the children left—after three and a half years most of the children still in care seem destined to remain so. He concludes that factors influencing the length of time spent in care should be predictable, so we may learn 'to counteract those forces

97

that create unintended tenure in care'.

Research indicates clearly that the first two years in foster-care—before attitudes harden or decay—are decisive in terms of both negative breakdown and positive rehabilitation.

Residential care and intermediate treatment

This section is short—partly because Beedell (1970) has written in this series on residential life with children; also because the 'caretakers' referred to throughout my book include residential staff. Other relevant literature includes Pugh (1968, chapter 6), Miller (1964), Balbernie (1966), Carlbach (1970), Brill and Thomas (1964), Burn (1956) who conveys Mr Lyward's ideas in poetical prose, Bettelheim (1950) who illustrates 'love for children' in relation to the routine events of daily communal life, and Dinnage and Pringle's review of research (1967 b). There are the collected papers of C. Winnicott (1964), Tod (1968 a and b) and Dockar Drysdale (1968). It may be worth comparing Burlingham and Freud's study (1944) of the case for and against residential nurseries with Flint's study (1967) of young children first in their deprived state, then during a period of residential care and later in adoptive or foster-homes. Articles include Davies (1963, 1966), A. Walker (1967), Hazel (1968), Parker (1967) advocating 'something more than this *catch-all-difficulties* function for residential care', and Parsons (1961) stressing the concern necessary for the staff's own children. Ingram's article (1961 b) is excellent on living together in the Children's Home; similarly a recent report on the Community Homes Project (HMSO, 1970).

To begin with an illustration from my own residential experience with delinquent adolescent girls:

One seasonal activity on the farm in late Spring was

incubating duck eggs, which requires skilful devotion
to detail over a period of 28 days. We offered local
duck-keepers a free service in order to fill our incubator
to capacity. In the first setting one year, we had almost
50 eggs from our own breeding unit (marked O for ours)
and about 25 eggs each from a neighbour, Mr H (marked
H) and from our chaplain, the local vicar (marked V).
All the parent-birds were white Aylesburys, producing
yellow ducklings. On the 7th day we tested the eggs
for fertility, turning each one separately over a beam
of light in a dark room, when a fertile egg shows up
its developing embryo as a spider-shape on the yolk,
and any infertile eggs are discarded. The H eggs gave
a reasonably good result of about 75% fertility; we
were delighted to discover the Os were 100% fertile,
but nonplussed that the Vs were totally infertile. We
turned on the light and blinked at each other, wanting
some explanation. One girl suggested, 'Perhaps the
Vicar don't know about that sort of thing' ... lively
discussion ensued (in which they recalled that V had
begotten at least 2 children).

Three weeks later we broke the news to the vicar,
and eased his possible disappointment with a gift of a
few of our own new ducklings. He accepted these gladly,
making in return the doubtful present of a further
batch of eggs, whose outcome he promised we could
keep. We went through the whole process again, with
much the same result—except that on the 7th day *one*
V egg did prove to be fertile. This became the apple
of our eye, tended with special care during 3 more
weeks. On the 28th day we had more than usual
excitement in watching the ducklings hatch: again
we counted a triumphant host of our own yellow
offspring, but the single V egg turned out to be a
black duckling. His mother earlier must have flown in
desperation to the town pond; however, he grew up
(named after the donor) a figure of importance on our
farm.

The participants in this modern parable gained in several

ways: a sense of achievement in carrying out the task (not least in feeling superior for once); increased confidence through acquiring specialised knowledge; identification with the deviant duckling who received special attention; and above all the shared experience strengthened our relationships with each other and with the local outside world. These elements are perhaps the essence of the therapeutic bonus possible in good residential care and in intermediate treatment. The worker is part of current events and has powerful influence for better or worse—e.g. the black duckling could have been purged as unwanted or the girls berated for disrespect to the vicar. Events may be planned or unplanned, treated explicitly or implicitly, but communication occurs within a real situation as it happens—in contrast to the fieldworker's more typical method of 'working backwards' with children after a crisis (see C. Winnicott, 1964, p. 9; also Kemp's account, 1971, of family treatment within the milieu of a residential centre for children, where parents are expected to play an active part for at least six hours a week, and where concrete situations are used 'on the spot' to assist parents in finding better ways of handling their child). Adopters and foster-parents ideally provide some special understanding extra to ordinary good parenting. Similarly, residential care has something to offer on two levels: a basic level of daily care (consisting at its lowest of holding and maintaining a group of bodies) plus the possibility of personal and social enhancement for children whose previous growth was interrupted, stunted or distorted.

The basic necessities of life, such as food, can be provided either as a dull routine or on both levels (e.g. Bettelheim, 1950, chapter 7, or Lowenburg, 1968). Administrators of Homes sometimes spend with over-generous unrealism on new carpets partly because they fail to see how else children can be compensated for past unhappiness. My view is that physical amenities can afford to be very ordinary—extra investment should be embodied in the personal and professional qualities of the staff. In turn the staff require special consideration because of the pressures of the work, including scope for privacy (accommodation enabling withdrawal when off duty instead of pretending to be a 'normal' family), support from fieldworkers, and consultation for their own development. Strained members of staff naturally tend to be restrictive or immersed in routine chores (fearful ones even to be cruel), and their own inner comfort affects not only the day-to-day atmosphere of the Home but their ability to help new children settle in. At the time of reception, the staff may unwittingly perform rituals—e.g. bathing, haircutting, changing clothes, dismissing personal belongings —designed to make the new child part of the set pattern, but which further undermine his already shaky sense of identity. The story of Samson symbolises the destructive effect of cutting a person's hair without his permission.

Intermediate treatment is given within a continuum ranging between the child's own home and institutional care; it may include casework, group work, community work, with chance for constructive links with schools and youth services. A father, whose adolescent son was receiving intermediate treatment, complained to the worker: 'It's supposed to be a punishment, but he's *enjoying* it!' Effective intermediate treatment is enjoyable—it does not assume that good character is built in proportion to the height of the mountain climbed by an unwilling child. In addition to group work, it gives scope for volunteers to help individual children through sharing a common interest with them. There is uncertainty in searching for new foster-parents to love a hypothetical child; it may prove more feasible sometimes to look for volunteers who are keen craftsmen, students, sportsmen (according to a child's expressed preference) and who are willing to let a relationship develop naturally out of a shared interest.

One aim is the growth of a young person's self-esteem through finding he can do something well besides make a nuisance of himself. Stevenson (1971) explores the implications of intermediate treatment being directed specifically towards children in trouble. She suggests as objectives: breaking out of roles into relationships between adults and children, and the right of each person to creative communication with himself.

So far I have made little specific mention of delinquent children, partly because their needs are like those of other young people, with an extra requirement of strongly-positive adult influence—a tough-minded kindness (which Bowlby has termed 'firm yet friendly intervention'). Ideas about delinquency tend to be confused or rigid, not only because research implies a bewilderingly multiple causation. Woodmansey (1971) provides convincing evidence that the chief cause (and effect) of delinquency has already been identified as hostility, but—because hostility in the delinquent arouses counter-hostility—'it can be shown that there will be an inevitable paradox in people's attitude towards delinquents, which seems almost bound to produce the very difficulties in understanding delinquency that we actually observe.' Woodmansey asserts that the family factors reliably predictive of delinquency are mainly related to parental hostility; and 'since the delinquent is convinced (whether mistakenly or not) that he is among enemies, treatment must depend on correcting this belief; whereas punishment can only serve to confirm it. It is urged that the solution of the problem of delinquency lies in prevention; and that this must be through effective parent guidance, which—since it needs to be therapeutic rather than instructional—will depend ultimately on more and better training of professional workers ...'

Woodmansey's work is referred to again in chapters 5 and 6. Meanwhile it endorses statements made, for example, by Irvine (1967) that 'hard-to-like' families need more than good enough parenting from the worker; as with the maladjusted child in residential care, 'they now need a parental figure who will be more understanding ... more patient than the majority of parents are, once earliest infancy is over'. And Wolff (1969) distils the challenge of residential care: 'All children who need to be looked after outside their own homes, for whatever reason, are children at risk. All have experienced unusual stresses ... The people who care for them are in a unique position ... to provide the kind of upbringing for each child that will make good his past deficiencies of care.'

School-children in difficulties

The remaining sections in this chapter will be shorter still, for reasons of space only. Since most children in this country attend school with some regularity, it is obviously one of the best places for preventive work, which requires closer co-operation between teachers and social workers than we have enjoyed hitherto.

First, *all* the children in this chapter may experience difficulties at school because they tend to see themselves as different from their peers; social workers do not want to make them appear more unusual by singling them out for attention at school, so must therefore communicate appropriately with teachers—ideally through a school social worker.

Second, consideration is needed for children in special boarding-schools: if they are in care as well as being physically or mentally handicapped, they may in some cases have no fixed abode but spend their years being shuttled back and forth.

Third, there is the majority of 'ordinary' school-children, some of whom experience large or small problems, especially perhaps in adolescence.

Fourth, there is a small group of children (reconsidered

in chapter 6) who find great difficulty in attending school at all. Kahn and Nursten (1968) present school-refusal as a psycho-social problem requiring a multi-disciplinary approach; they discuss methods ranging from typical treatment within child guidance clinics to behaviour therapy.

School counsellors are specially trained, after gaining experience as qualified teachers, and are concerned with educational/vocational/personal guidance. Jones (1970) describes an experiment in counselling adolescent school-girls, and appropriate co-ordination between counsellor, parents, form tutor and external social workers. Her referrals came not through teachers but through running a series of small group discussions on human relationships for all third year girls, who could then request individual counselling if they wished. In a form of thirty girls, it was found that about ten asked for counselling—of these about six may have 'normal' developmental problems, two or three may have rather more serious problems, and one or two may require referral to child guidance or 'children's department'. Clegg and Megson (1968) estimate that at least ten per cent of children require preventative help within the school. Collected papers (eds Craft, Raynor and Cohen, 1967) review the home-school link in the sociology of education, describing ways of achieving closer contact between parents and teachers, and of using the school as a focal point in the local community.

Klein and Ross (1965) study the role-transition of the five-year-old school-child and the impact of school-entry on the whole family, which may be eased through parents' discussion groups. Rabinowitz (1969) describes flexible, research-based co-operation in a multi-purpose school for handicapped children, and Greenway (1966) gives a detailed account of helping severely disturbed children to learn through her and from each other. Pringle (1965, 1969) stresses the importance of early prevention of language/

educational difficulties among emotionally and culturally deprived children, and the need for remedial education, in its widest sense, from pre-school years onwards, with teachers as potential 'general practitioners' in child and family life. Caplan (1961, pp. 197-201) shows how a mental health consultant/social worker can help teachers, whose own personal problems echo in the children with whom they experience special difficulty, in discussion groups which focus explicitly on how to help specific children.

Immigrant children

It can be a bitter struggle for immigrant children to acquire a clear sense of identity and self-esteem : their problems may be greater in passing through 'normal' maturational crises, and vastly magnified for coloured children of mixed parentage who may also be illegitimate and in care. A small group of neighbouring coloured children visit my home weekly—their extreme vulnerability and jealousy of each other's grades of skin-colour and hair-kinkiness tend to reduce their immediate enjoyment of pleasant experiences; their uncertainties about colour frequently arise indirectly—e.g. on first going out to pick blackberries, they could hardly believe the black berries were really more desirable than the unripe but 'prettier red and green ones'. It is meaningless to generalise about coloured children : therefore the relevant literature provides only faint guide-lines for consideration of individual families.

Morrish (1971) portrays three main cultural and religious backgrounds of West Indian, Indian and Pakistani groups. Kitzinger (1969) discusses communication with immigrant mothers :

> We must be willing to be taught by those we are seeking to teach ... What we have to learn is not simply a series of quaint customs ... but the very root and life of what being a member of another culture means. It

is only thus that we can begin to utilise values already operating and meaningful, both to understand something of what people's lives mean to them, the way they see themselves and—if we are trying to assist them to adjust to new challenges in their environment—to help them towards necessary changes.

Articles on the problems of coloured/half-coloured children in care include R. Jenkins (1963), Antrobus (1964), Davies (1967), Holman (1968), Shapiro (1968), Foren and Batta (1970); Triseliotis (1963) discusses immigrant school-children, and A. Walker (1968) disturbed immigrant children. Barnardo's (1966) reports on its work in relation to racial integration. Fitzherbert (1967) has already been mentioned in the foster-care section, and Raynor (1970) in the section on adoption. Social workers who are themselves coloured make an extremely important contribution, with the slight risk that they, who also suffer from sentimental discrimination, may naturally prefer us to be neutrally firm rather than exaggeratedly tolerant. Burns (1971) mentions the strong ambivalence of his own race towards white people, and advises that groups of children evenly divided between white and coloured are freer to gravitate where they choose, thereby arousing less prejudice and anxiety latent in residential staff.

Holman (ed. 1970, pp. 151-2) summarises some of the social disadvantages of immigrant families with low incomes in over-crowded dwellings in areas often characterised by over-crowded schools. Hutchinson (1969) discusses ethical problems which social workers face in situations of culture conflict, where it is hard to decide whether a child will find long-term public care less hurtful than remaining in his own home. I think the most vulnerable groups of coloured children are these:

1. The many babies/pre-school children farmed out in apparently casual good faith to a series of 'poor white' families (see Ellis, 1971).

2. Children left behind in their native land who are sent for at puberty for their potential usefulness (almost a slave trade in reverse) but who may later cause angry disappointment if they fail to settle in a strange family here.
3. Near-delinquent children who may be punished severely by anxious parents with foreign child-rearing attitudes which expect nine-year-olds to be highly responsible and not to be 'rude'.
4. Children of mixed unions (whose white mothers may have deserted the family) who grow up in care; who need special care of skin and hair, to be helped to make the most of their physical appearance, their education and their relationships with adults of any colour.

Handicapped children

Instead of attempting here to cover the great range of handicaps which children may suffer (see Kershaw, 1961), a few ideas are extracted from relevant studies, mainly considering children who are mentally or physically handicapped, but also mentioning the disturbance caused by physical and emotional sickness in families. The report of a working party with the National Children's Bureau (ed. Younghusband *et al.*, 1970) considers broadly—from the viewpoint of medicine, education, social work—aspects of 'living with handicap', but had to exclude socially disadvantaged children, young drug-addicts and delinquents. The report emphasises that the needs of the handicapped child and his family are exactly like those of any other family, 'but to meet them is far harder because man has to strive to do what nature accomplishes effortlessly for those who develop normally'. Though 'normal' adolescence is not effortless, the report mentions a surprising failure to recognise the acute problems of isolation from their peers which confront many handicapped adolescents. Having enlarged on the fallacy of labels and the fact that a simple, single handicap is rare—partly because it impinges cumulatively in several directions—the report stresses the importance of early diagnosis, early learning, continuous assessment, of keeping the physical, emotional, educational and social needs of the child in constant balance, using an inter-disciplinary approach, with the parents as participants in the team. The role of voluntary organisations is vital, and the poverty or otherwise of supporting social services directly affects the parents' ability to persevere

These ideas should offset the tendency to treat a handicapped child purely in terms of an obvious label, though it seems hard for 'normal' people to find an appropriate balance between recognising and denying differences imposed by disability. Often the family is expected to respond with great nobility of spirit; alternatively we anticipate that parents and child are certain to have deep guilt-feelings which must be aired. Pringle and Fiddes (1970), studying the challenge presented by thalidomide children, find evidence to suggest that families do tend either to cope heroically or to prove unequal to the tremendous strain. The families' sense of grief and loss is often insufficiently recognised; it seems acceptable for them to voice guilt, but not the anger which is part of grief and which may be directed at would-be helpful services. In a quarter of the families with a thalidomide child, one or both parents showed symptoms of emotional strain. Similarly, Tizard and Grad's survey (1961) of 250 families with mentally subnormal children living at home and in institutions showed a high incidence of physical and mental stress in the mothers. McMichael's study (1971) of physically handicapped children in a small primary school shows the emotional hazards for every member of each family. Hewett and Newsons' account (1970) of 180 cerebral palsied children in their own homes makes vivid reading as the mothers (like the Newsons' Nottingham mothers, 1963, 1968) tell their experiences in their own words.

This account of Hewett and the Newsons highlights the very individual response to the experience of living with handicap: many of the families lead quite ordinary lives in spite of inconvenient housing and lack of outside support—one inevitable difference is caused by their need for considerable contact with medical and social services. More than half the sample found their family doctor helpful (depending partly on his ability to convey himself as an ally) but a more qualified welcome was given to social workers of various kinds, partly because the workers had limited resources available such as day care and (the mothers felt) limited specialised knowledge. To the question, 'What is it about your child you find hardest to cope with?', the mothers gave a wide range of individual responses. The authors felt it inappropriate to try to measure parental acceptance of handicap, which can only glibly be termed 'acceptable'. If parents of ordinary children are often shocked to discover themselves capable of hostile feelings, then 'the handicapped child will present his parents with a situation which is quite outside their ordinary hopes and expectations', and may arouse strong feelings of fear, resentment and self-reproach. Just over half the mothers said their child's condition had not been explained to them; some had found out a good deal for themselves, others preferred not to know too much—a large number felt the news had been given adequately. Furneaux (1969) also discusses the need to give parents of mentally subnormal children opportunities to assimilate the confirmation of handicap, and she draws attention to the fact that 'community care' tends to be provided at the expense of straining the family actually afflicted.

These studies suggest the need for far more listening to those who live with handicap—listening in order both to give the necessary practical support and to respond to the actual feelings being expressed. Olshansky (1965) writes of the chronic sorrow of having a mentally subnormal child. It is the very long-term nature of the predicament and fear of the abnormal which taxes neighbourly goodwill. The National Children's Bureau is producing a series of studies in child development ('normal' and handicapped), including Dinnage's review (1971) of ten years of research on the handicapped child, and the first of a series of 'spotlight' reference books (Parfit, 1971) which deals with physical and mental assessment; there is also Pringle's article (1970) on the policy implications of child development studies.

This section finishes with brief consideration of children handicapped in other ways. I have not attempted to list the wide variety of behaviour problems exhibited by uneasy children (see R C C A Review, 1962, for a simple A B C) because the form each problem takes, whether it be stealing, soiling, drug-addiction or eating the stair carpet, is relevant mainly in the distress it causes both child and caretaker. In my view, treatment lies not in any specific prescription for each symptom, but in the emotional climate prevailing in the home. Reference can be made to C. Winnicott (1968, pp. 73-9), Woodmansey (1966 b, 1969); and Burton (1968) who studies three vulnerable groups of children—those involved in road accidents, sexually assaulted and asthmatic children—and who discusses whether their observed behaviour can be seen as attempts to overcome conflicts with close adults. Anthony and Koupernik (1970) edit papers on childhood problems within the family, including several about children who eat too much or too little. Axline's classic account (1966) of her therapeutic relationship with Dibs has a miniature counterpart in Prestage's story (1964) of Kim.

Irvine (1964) drew attention to children at risk through having a parent recently admitted to a psychiatric hospital, and Rutter's work (1966) begins to answer her concern.

Lloyd (1965) describes casework help for a child preparing herself for the ordeal of facial surgery; Daniel (1964) describes casework with sick children and their parents. Morrissey (1965) discusses ways of easing death anxiety in children with a fatal illness—children as young as three and a half years old are thought capable of experiencing and expressing fear of death symbolically; older boys tend to act out their fear and older girls to become depressed.

Ill-treated and neglected children

It is important to study the 'battered child syndrome' for several reasons: first, though the number of known cases each year may be small, the suffering involved is enormous and passes from one generation to the next like other parent-child problems. Secondly, because such desperate behaviour in parent-figures provokes extreme reactions (incredulous/punitive/sentimental) in everybody concerned, workers should think out general policy before decisions have to be made about a specific child. Thirdly, understanding of extreme adult hostility may help both in treating its milder manifestations and in avoiding groundless suspicion of its occurrence.

Treatment of parental hostility is considered in chapter 5; meanwhile it is best to visualise battering as part of a continuum which includes less sensational but perhaps equally harmful interaction with children. There is a danger that current preoccupation with battered babies may allow unbruised children suffering similar hostility to go unnoticed. Kempe *et al.* (1962) first used the term 'battered child syndrome' to characterise 'a clinical condition in young children who have received serious physical abuse, generally from a parent or foster-parent'. These children are usually under three years old, particularly dependent on parent-figures; they may have severe multiple injuries—causing death or permanent handicap to some; others recover in hospital and may unwittingly be discharged to a dangerous home environment where they are injured again. Parents under suspicion are usually unable to offer a convincing explanation for the injuries.

The problem is being studied, notably by Helfer and Kempe in America and by the NSPCC team first led by Joan Court in Britain. Helfer and Kempe's first book (1968) contains papers on historical, medical, legal aspects; a most useful part being the psychiatric study of abusive parents by Steele and Pollock. They studied and treated sixty families intensively during a period of five and a half years.

> At first sight the group had little in common but appeared like any random cross-section of the population. However, there proved to be a clear, consistent behaviour pattern in that these parents expected a great deal from their children prematurely. They were unsure of their own identity and misperceived their child's helplessness; '... when he cried all the time it meant he didn't love me, so I hit him' (aged 3 weeks). They often showed a punitive self-righteousness—'Children have to be taught proper respect', through exaggerated measures used to 'discipline' the child at an inappropriately early age. There was clear evidence that the parents had been treated similarly themselves; even if not violently handled, they had experienced a sense of constant parental criticism. Also it seemed they had all been deprived of basic 'mothering', without necessarily lacking attention in the sense of being kept clean, fed and trained. They were not entirely punitive, but likely to hit when under stress caused by the child's demands or by his unresponsiveness; when frustrated, criticised or provoked by their marriage partner.

The same kind of pattern is emerging in British studies (Hughes 1967, Court 1969, Skinner and Castle 1969), of a critical, unselfconfident, possibly self-righteous, socially isolated person, perhaps with a strong marriage tie based on great unmet needs, and little hope anywhere except in the baby. Three elements precipitate attack: a potentially abusive parent-figure, a particular child who is seen in some way as awkward/unloving (siblings may be spared injury but are at some risk) and a critical situation. Treatment is difficult; the worker must first meet his own feelings about hostility in order to empathise with the parent as a hurt child, who requires a new experience of good parenting which can then begin to spread to the next generation. The worker must show concern for the parent's suffering, not only in words, but in attitude and availability.

Decisions about the future safety of injured children are difficult: legal (or other) punishment of the parents is obviously destructive; a period of enforced separation for the child is usually the best protection for all concerned, and the parents may be able to see this as a helpful step towards reunion whilst they accept treatment. In assessing whether the child is still at risk, two favourable signs are: first, when the child seems more natural with the parents, less watchful, less polite, begins to lead a life of his own and can risk being ordinarily naughty; secondly, if the parent finds satisfaction in the worker which gradually spreads more widely, there is a less dangerous investment in the child. One mother said towards the end of treatment, 'I'm listening to my little girl the way you listen to me. She's a real person to me now and I enjoy her ...'

Helfer and Kempe are producing a new book (1971); meanwhile Helfer (1970) outlines a plan for protection through a 'child-abuse center'. The main change in ideas seems to result through believing it impracticable to offer all child-abusers the necessary skilled psychiatric/casework help. Helfer's alternative solution is to make the home safe for the child's return by attacking the wall of social isolation which surrounds the parents. This is done 'by bombarding the wall with substitute mothers' in the form of friendly, partially-trained volunteers who are vigorously supported by a therapeutic team in the background. 'We assist the parents in developing friends and gradually teach them how to ask for and accept help from others.' The child's safe return home may be planned in three to six months in 70 per cent of the reported cases—otherwise, Helfer says, parental rights should be severed after a year.

This idea may prove practicable, but to me it seems ludicrous to 'bombard' a batterer, even with kindness, and I still see casework help as the most effective method. Certainly our sympathetic understanding of such parents should not prevent realistic decisions to sever parental ties in extreme cases, in order to free the child to grow up elsewhere. Davies and Jorgensen (1970) tell the story of one battered child who had to say goodbye to his parents and who was gradually given sufficient confidence to settle into an adoptive home (see also Kadushin, 1970). At present a child in this country has to be badly hurt at least once before the battering syndrome is recognised. The basic question surely is that of *prevention* at a stage even before the health visitor may notice small bruises round a baby's mouth. Prevention is sought through general awareness of the problem of parental hostility, and by learning to predict potentially abusive behaviour with some accuracy in discussion with expectant mothers, expectant adopters, prospective foster-parents—any of whom might show uneasiness in advance about the child's demands or have strange ideas about 'disciplining' a baby, particularly in toilet-training him.

Finally, is there any difference between parents who actively ill-treat their children and those who passively neglect them? Research is inconclusive—e.g. Young (1964) makes a clear distinction between the two whereas Fontana *et al.* (1963) suggest 'a situation ranging from the deprivation of food, clothing, shelter and parental love to incidents in which children are physically abused and mistreated by an adult ...' Possibly battering parents have more in common as a group (even the horribly active nature of their behaviour means that one has something to work with if one can reach them) than neglectful parents whose behaviour may result from depression, ill-health, lack of inner and outer resources (see Halliwell 1969, Younghusband 1965, or Philp 1963). I have an image of a battering mother combing her child's hair with harsh thoroughness, whereas a neglectful mother may not even bother to comb her own hair. However, battering incidents tend to be triggered off by environmental stresses—therefore treatment should include practical, material aid. Clearly both battering and neglectful parents have tremendous unmet needs of their own, leading the former to make unrealistic demands of the child and the latter partially to ignore the child's needs.

It is probably irrelevant to attempt to categorise troubled parent-figures—effective methods of *helping* them are considered in the following chapter.

5

Helping parents to help their children

What are you crying for? said an Angry Parent to a Child, whom he had sharply and harshly rebuked. You have snuffed the candle too close, replied I—and can you wonder, that it gutters?

(Coleridge)

Anything which is at variance and enmity with itself is not likely to be in union or harmony with any other thing.

(Plato)

To help children we frequently must first help parents. A deprived parent who receives understanding and help may gain in capacity to give understanding and help. The parent who fails frequently is the parent who has been failed, hence ... the social worker and agency should not repeat his unloving parent through aligning with the children versus him ... and through restrictive services given grudgingly, without understanding his frustration at the limits of the giving.

(Charlotte Towle: *Helping*)

Coleridge's reaction to an angry parent, who seemed to

expect his child to accept harsh correction with an obedient smile, is not unlike the way in which modern social workers are often tempted to speak to hostile parent-figures. 'Of course your child is upset by your unkindness —at most you may be able to frighten him into superficial obedience, but in the long run you will turn him into an angry person like yourself.' Sometimes it may be necessary to ask a parent or caretaker to be easier towards his children, but only King Canute would expect waves of anger to abate by order. We need Plato's understanding that a person who shows enmity towards others is usually at variance with himself. This leads logically to Towle's belief that such parents need *help*—not criticism, exhortation, punishment, snubs or rejection. They need help both in their own right and in the interests of their children. In this chapter particularly I am thinking of parents and caretakers interchangeably, and any of the examples given may be relevant to natural parents, residential staff, foster-parents, teachers or other adults in daily charge of children.

The chapter divides to some extent into two sections: considering first, parent-figures who live *with* children; secondly, parent-figures who are *separated* from their children.

Parent-figures living with children

Mrs Hill, an obese woman who had not previously recognised the fact that she was pregnant with her 7th child, was referred by her G P when the baby was actually due because arrangements had to be made for the care of the other 6 children during the confinement in hospital. The worker spent much of 2 days trying to make plans with the Hill family, which apparently was usually able to organise its own affairs (and then the new baby arrived on the 3rd day). Initially Mrs Hill was in a state of shock and unpreparedness, unable to co-operate sensibly in making plans. She demanded at first that the 6 children should be accommodated in a Children's Home for the 10 days but, on hearing this was impossible, she stipulated that all 6 children should be placed together in one foster-home. The children had not required reception into care during the previous confinements because their maternal grandmother had come from some distance away to look after them in their own home. An s o s to the grandmother on this occasion was met, according to Mrs Hill, by blank refusal to help. The children's father worked on night shifts; slept during a small part of long days at home and seemed very capable, so the worker thought the best solution would be to find a suitable neighbour willing to sleep in the Hills' home for 9 nights. This was the plan finally agreed upon (which subsequently proved successful) but not until Mrs Hill during the 2 preliminary days had transferred to the previously-unknown worker her feelings of helpless, angry dependence upon her own mother, whom she felt had 'slapped her down'. It was immaterial that the worker was unmarried and somewhat younger than Mrs Hill : what did matter was that the worker gave Mrs Hill a brief but real experience of 'good mothering' without being overwhelmed by the pressures in the situation. The worker's response to Mrs Hill's own acute needs was the major factor in avoiding the emergency reception into short-term care of 6 children.

The last part of Towle's statement is also important : adult clients who have themselves suffered deprivation, failure and hostility tend to ask more of us than we can hope to give in terms of time, understanding and other agency resources. The worker's discomfort, when faced by an importunate client, may lead to withdrawal or to 'restrictive services given grudgingly'. But for the worker to recognise openly with the client 'his frustration at the limits of the giving' is in itself a therapeutic experience.

In other words, the very thing which often mars worker-client transactions can be used instead to further the relationship: the client is comforted through realising that the worker is not only aware of his frustration and annoyance but remains concerned to offer whatever help is possible. Mayer and Timms' research (1970) studied clients speaking of their experience as consumers of a casework service. A number of these clients expressed dissatisfaction: sometimes apparently because of a clash of perspective with the worker—e.g. when the client saw the problem as being the entire fault of the spouse or child whom the worker was expected to 'sort out' promptly, or when the client naturally resented her request for material aid resulting in exploration of her social history. Clearly some dissatisfaction can be avoided if workers use commonsense and imagination: however, I am not concerned here to argue this point so much as to say that often dissatisfaction is inevitable; that in turn it leads to anger and frustration, and that these feelings are best met rather than politely ignored.

Kay (1967) suggests that foster-parents should be regarded as important resources to be conserved and developed. He believes it is possible to use foster-parents who have areas of vulnerability, provided there is careful selection, preparation and placement, and provided the worker can safeguard the child through enabling foster-parents to express their complex reactions to the experience of fostering. In chapter 2 I mentioned a distressed foster-mother once saying resentfully to me, 'Of course you are always on the foster-child's side'. My reply—'I hope we're all on the same side, Mrs Smith'—was not helpful, because it quite ignored the needs of Mrs Smith herself. *Her* problem was a growing desperation over her foster-child Jill's stealing and jealousy, coupled with annoyance over my inability to acknowledge that her exasperation was natural in the circumstances. *My* problem was mounting apprehension that Mrs Smith would reject Jill, who had already been rejected more than once before. Although I listened patiently to Mrs Smith's anxiety, I must have feared that any open appreciation from me of her plight would merely give her the necessary reinforcement and courage to demand Jill's removal. Also I was so preoccupied in considering Jill's dangerous position, that I was not really aware that Mrs Smith's immediate anger was actually directed at me, for being so uncompromisingly 'on Jill's side'.

This kind of situation, where a parent or caretaker is spilling over with accumulations of resentment about a child, is extremely common in family casework. Unfortunately it is also common for the worker to respond as I did—to plead for the child instead of considering the caretaker's problem. And such pleading administers a double snub; it not only ignores the caretaker's predicament but implies that these negative feelings would be blameworthy if they were recognised. It would have eased Mrs Smith immediately had I recognised openly her natural frustration with me. (It is preferable to voice her resentment as 'frustration' rather than 'anger', as the worker's use of the word 'anger' may sound more accusatory than accepting.) It seemed likely that part of Mrs Smith's distress stemmed from her own childish temptations towards stealing and jealousy. However, it would not have been appropriate to point this out to a foster-mother; nor would it be very helpful to share similar insight with any parent-figure, even if one had a clearly-defined casework function. At some stage it might be worthwhile for the worker to suggest that all children and even grown-ups sometimes feel jealous of other people's affections and possessions, as this may help the caretaker to forgive herself as well as the child. But it is secondary to the importance of meeting Mrs Smith's obvious problem: 'I'm worried to death by Jill, and this official doesn't begin to understand how I feel, she's only concerned about Jill.' (The worker who says out-right, 'I think I understand how you feel', possibly sounds more banal to fellow social workers than he does to clients. But such a comment is potentially irritating and presumptuous, and it may be preferable to say something specifically relevant which conveys implicit empathic understanding.)

It is also helpful sometimes to tell caretakers that children who have previously been failed by their adults are bound to be difficult, and that awkward behaviour is no reflection on the qualities of the current caretaker but rather a hopeful sign of testing whether renewed trust is possible. However, such explanation is again of secondary value in comparison with acknowledging that the testing-out is hard to bear and that it may cause the caretaker to feel the worker has deliberately landed her with an impossible task. It may seem insincere at first sight for the worker to concentrate on the viewpoint of whomsoever he happens to be with at the moment, but in reality it is far more genuinely effective to respond to the actual pressure of feeling in the person present than it is to appeal to a troubled person to consider someone else's predicament. (The troubled person will become more considerate as soon as she is less immersed in her own troubles.) Again, if the worker is to communicate helpfully with the person present, he needs to voice barriers from the client's viewpoint and not from his own (though these need private thought). It is of little use saying, 'I find it difficult to help you when you're so mistrustful of my goodwill', or 'I hope we're all on the same side'. Mrs Smith may gain some confidence through hearing something like: 'It's extra difficult for you if you see me on Jill's side—not realising how hard it is on you ...' (Such remarks sound forced or foolish unless they come naturally, with genuine concern, in the worker's own words.)

The word 'aggression' looms large in the vocabulary of social workers, but it seems conceivable that we pay insufficient attention to the extremely vicious circle caused by parental hostility. Bowlby's work is usually seen in terms of the importance of continuity of care; however, Bowlby did not only stress the dangers of uprooting a small child: he also emphasised positively the child's need for a warm, intimate relationship with a parent-figure 'in which both find satisfaction and enjoyment'. Ainsworth (1962) points out, as mentioned above in chapter 1, that the term 'maternal deprivation' includes *distortion* in the character of parent-child interaction without respect to its quantity. A considerable body of evidence shows that parental hostility has a particularly harmful effect on a child's development, and that the distortion (when untreated) perpetuates itself from generation to generation. The lullabies in chapter 1 show that the negative side of parental ambivalence has many guises—it may occur as blatant bad-temper, or emerge as a self-righteous duty to punish and control naughtiness; it may nag, scold, withhold, over-protect, or over-compensate materially, restrict, taunt ... It may hurt deliberately, inconsistently or accidentally; it may be very frequent or reserved for specific misbehaviour; it is usually ambivalent, alternating with some measure of affection ... But whether it is intended for the 'child's own good', shown in hot anger or with cold calculation, hostility is extremely frightening and harmful to the child.

Some people think that punishment and 'mental cruelty' rarely occur in today's permissive society, in the same way that other ostriches believe the Welfare State has overcome real poverty. Social workers tend to become acclimatised to other people's painful situations—a student may be shocked on first meeting a wife who complains of regular beatings from her husband; experienced workers may believe that such a marriage is more tolerable (even quite excitingly enjoyable) than it appears, and is virtually the norm in certain circles. Clients vary in their resilience, but surely no worker can pretend that children enjoy much confidence in living with parent-figures who treat them with more unkindness than consistent affection. Parents may complain that the child is 'hardened to punishment', but he is more likely to have been driven into numb defiance and impotent rage. Woodmansey's paper (1969) studies case details of an unselected, consecutive series of seventy teenage psychiatric patients referred to him with a variety of problems—e.g. depression, anxiety state, psychosomatic illness, delinquency. Disturbed children are certainly difficult to live with, and parent-figures easily rationalise the need for strict control but, as Woodmansey asserts, true morality depends not on fear of punishment but on friendly feelings and positive identifications. He thinks that serious problems of adolescence are generally found either to be exacerbations of previously existing childhood disorders, or to be manifestations of current clashes with overtly hostile adults.

Of these seventy consecutive adolescents, aged between thirteen and seventeen years on referral, Woodmansey considered that sixty-four had an established disorder and six were healthy subjects reacting to current conflicts with adults. In the total series of seventy patients, only four were found whose parents appeared to be on fairly friendly terms with each other and with their children (and one of the four had a punitive teacher); fifty-four of the sixty-four patients with an established disorder had experienced severe punishment (e.g. thrashings) or intense parental hostility, while a further six were involved in the threats and recriminations of parents who were extremely hostile to each other.

The paper (1969) also reviews Bowlby's well-known study (1946) of forty-four juvenile thieves: although seventeen of these had experienced prolonged early separation and eleven had had recent traumatic experiences, Woodmansey finds evidence in the study that *at least* thirty-three of the forty-four young people were victims of extremely hostile parents or guardians. This suggests that we should be *at least* as alert to signs of parental aggression in family casework and in preventive work generally as we are preoccupied with situations involving separation. Elsewhere (1966 a, 1966 b, 1971) Woodmansey enlarges on his hypothesis that childhood psychogenic illnesses of various kinds can be regarded as the result of specific responses (i.e. fear, retaliation or self-attack) to the hostility of parent-figures. The hypothesis provides a logical basis for prevention, and for treatment of children or parents or both. He sees the main aim of 'parent guidance' as being simple in principle though sometimes hard in practice—'it is just to help parents to be nice to their children'. When adolescents have developed their own inner conflicts, they are likely to need treatment in their own right, but very often the alleviation of the parents' hostility alone is sufficient treatment.

Here is an example of casework help for a parent; it is relevant also to Mrs Smith and to very many other troubled parent-figures.

A twelve-year-old boy, Michael, was referred to a family guidance clinic by his G P as having been 'difficult to manage for some years'. At his first *and only* appointment, Michael seemed a very resentful, uncommunicative boy. His mother, Mrs Lacey, was also seen—'a rather old-fashioned, respectable woman, very anxious and hostile'. From the mother's account it seemed there was a vicious circle of hostility in the family. Mr Lacey, a lorry driver, dissociated himself from the family problems. Michael had recently been in trouble with the police for stealing, which was a great shock to the family, and he appeared to be suffering further strain as an intelligent boy attending a predominantly middle-class school away from his own district. Michael and his younger brother, John, frequently had violent quarrels in which Mrs Lacey feared they would cause each other serious injury. After the initial interview with Michael and with his mother, it was decided that the psychiatric social worker should offer casework help to Mrs Lacey. No immediate plans were made for the psychiatrist to see Michael again until it became clearer whether help for the mother alone would improve the interpersonal relationships within the family, and thus help Michael indirectly.

The social worker during the next two and a half years had about thirty interviews with Mrs Lacey, virtually all of these being home visits by appointment (during school hours when other members of the family were only occasionally met in passing). No dramatic changes occurred, though it seems clear from the record that some of the parental pressure on Michael was reduced at a very early stage: there were apparently no further delinquent episodes, and it gradually transpired that Michael was on better terms with both parents, working successfully at school and enjoying leisure activities. These aspects emerge without emphasis in the record, interspersed with ups and downs; the focus of sympathy throughout was upon Mrs Lacey's own problems, and one's main impression is of the worker's willingness to persevere in offering friendly support to a very troubled woman. The worker engaged in a long, slow, difficult process of meeting Mrs Lacey's hostility without retaliation or withdrawal: this was possible partly because of the worker's previous experience of the effectiveness of such relationships. Critics may think that some other method (e.g. behaviour therapy for Michael or the involvement of all four members in conjoint family therapy) would have produced quicker results, but surely thirty hours is an economic use of scarce resources when it proves helpful to the whole family.

In the early interviews, Mrs Lacey seemed isolated, depressed and resigned to circumstances which were almost intolerable to her. She saw her husband and Michael (and John to a lesser extent) as bad, violent, delinquent males, and herself as trying hopelessly to enforce some sense and order in the face of their cruel ingratitude. She described her husband as having been brought up very strictly (herself rather less so) and she felt he had reacted against this by being too soft and evasive with their sons (thereby implying that they deserved strict treatment). She dwelt on the emptiness of her marriage and Mr Lacey's 'dirty' sexual behaviour towards her and other women. She was extremely ambivalent towards the worker, at first showing indirect hostility and gradually becoming able to express this more directly, particularly in criticising the help she was being given. The worker could have focused on various intriguing areas of stress within the extended family, but concentrated instead on offering Mrs Lacey herself a new kind of relationship in which the mother's hostility could be met helpfully at first hand.

More important than the plain ventilation of anger in a vacuum is the way in which it is met when it does emerge: if it can be met over a period of time by a worker who recognises it openly yet is neither hurt by it nor hurtful in reply, the anger does seem slowly to evaporate and lose its destructive power. This case re-emphasises a worker's helpfulness in empathising with the client's subjective feelings instead of commenting objectively on the situation. If the worker had argued, or colluded in agreeing that other members of the family were bad, Mrs Lacey would probably not have been able to withdraw her own projections. Mrs Lacey, having started by seeing herself as the injured party, gradually disclosed her own 'badness' and violence; sometimes her strict, punitive side alternated in reproaching the worker's lenience. While the worker remained constant, Mrs Lacey slowly found a balance in asserting herself more positively, less restrictively, and she became more friendly not only to the worker but towards her husband and sons. None of this happened neatly or miraculously, but it is the clear pattern underlying an undramatic record.

The above section of this chapter has emphasised the need for helping parent-figures in difficulties to be on better terms with their children because it seems the importance of such work is not always sufficiently recognised. It is relevant to very many children in a wide range of situations and special circumstances. Fear, anger, anxiety and depression chase each other's tails in troubled families, spoiling relationships inside and outside the home. Inseparable from emotional factors are physical aspects such as housing, food, employment—and problems such as rent arrears, debt, ill-health, affliction of body and estate. These have not been dwelt upon here because their importance is more apparent, even though our ability to help families to tackle these problems is often makeshift, scratching the surface. Two further questions remain: one is the time element in family casework; the second is the social worker's dilemma in finding some balance between acting as a helping person and as an agent of social control.

Little research exists in this country on the relative effectiveness of brief and extended casework. Reid and Shyne's study in New York (1969) compared the results of two types of casework for interpersonal problems: *planned short-term treatment* (eight interviews) and *continued service*, open-ended as to time. Their research sample consisted of middle-income families, voluntarily seeking agency help with clearly perceived problems in marital or parent-child transactions. Their major finding was that planned short-term treatment yielded more progress than long-continued service; also this progress was assessed as equally durable. Apparently the workers were more active in the short-term cases, and the clients possibly more co-operative through knowing in advance that treatment would be brief and clearly directed towards limited goals. The results of the study (which may not apply generally in Britain) are very acceptable, in rather the same way that foster-care has been popular not least because it is financially cheaper than residential care.

Reid and Shyne's research will encourage busy social workers in their short-term interventions; it confirms former experience of crisis-situations, and the value of the two-day upheaval with Mrs Hill (though that was not formally planned) earlier in this chapter. Family case-workers also know from experience that one evening's work, in visiting the family of an adolescent referred as being beyond control, may often restore sufficient communication within the family to enable it to function independently. Reid and Shyne's study does not invalidate the help given to Mrs Lacey; it is doubtful whether the outcome there could have been achieved in a shorter time. Nor does it affect the fact that multi-problem families may require outside support for a generation or longer, though the help given may be concentrated during critical phases and minimal in between. Bruce's spider remains a valid symbol.

The second question is that of finding some balance between friendly permissiveness and firm control. There is not space here to explore my doubts as to whether society can legitimately expect to use social workers as external watch-dogs and disciplinarians (see Plant, 1970). At the same time, social workers clearly possess considerable professional and personal authority, and therefore clients have opportunities to experience a new, positive relationship with Authority in the form of a friendly human being (see Foren and Bailey, 1968). The hope in this chapter for friendly relationships between workers and parent-figures, and thus between the latter and their children, is certainly not advocating weak sentimentality. 'It is a curious thing (Bowlby says, 1958) how many intelligent adults think that the only alternative to letting a child run wild is to inflict punishment. A policy of firm yet friendly intervention when a child is doing something we wish to stop not only creates far less bitterness but in the long run is far more effective.'

Perhaps a partial answer to the worker's dilemma is found through amending a phrase used in chapter 1, where it was suggested that a basic social need of any child is 'sufficient *firmness to prevent* his hurting himself or others'. Here is a much more positive way of looking at this same need: '*parental strength to protect* him from harming himself or others'. There is a small but subtle difference in the two phrases. With a parent-figure who is fearful, uncertain and tempted to be punitive, it can be dangerous to advocate an attitude of 'firmness to prevent'. But an attitude in the worker of 'parental strength to protect' is helpful for all kinds of children and clients, ranging from the most timid handicapped child to the most violently acting-out delinquent of any age. Therefore, in seeking to help uncomfortable parent-figures (when the worker may be pressurised by society's over-riding concern for the child) it is most effective for the worker to think of his role as that of a 'good parent' to the child within the troubled parent-figure.

Parent-figures separated from their children

When a parent, for whatever length of time, hands over the care of his child, caretakers tend to concentrate on the child to the exclusion of the parent. Almost by conspiracy we imply that the parent has forfeited his right to play a continuing part in the child's life; he may complicate an already difficult situation and he can best co-operate by keeping quiet in the background. Even highly competent parents tend to feel superfluous when entrusting their child to the experts (e.g. in hospital or at school). But the attitude: 'You couldn't cope, so leave it to us,' is more marked towards parents who have partially failed in their role. Their rejoinder may be: 'You took him away, so you can get on with it.' Such parents cannot on their own initiative find a balance between giving and receiving appropriate help for their separated child. It is only too easy for them to adopt an 'all or nothing' attitude: to opt out completely, to clamour possessively, to interfere obstructively, to appear like a bad fairy at the most awkward moment, to disappear when wanted (e.g. to sign some consent form) and generally to show themselves incapable of carrying through consistent plans.

Caretaking agencies, by ignoring the parents' distress, may actually allow their alienation from the child and subsequently use this in evidence against them (see George, 1970, p. 220). It is intolerable for unselfconfident parents to hover impotently, awaiting opportunities to share crumbs of their shattered role. Virtually any parent is aware when he is valued by those who have taken over the child, and he usually responds accordingly. Putative fathers are traditionally perhaps the most evasive figures of all, resentful of being sought largely for their name, intentions and money, but they frequently prove remarkably concerned; respectful recognition of their ambiguous position is far more effective than any officious moralising. Many parents, including those of handicapped children, may have been driven through desperation to take up an extreme stance of rejection, but recognition of their plight may enable them to resume some measure of responsibility. Most people, including unsupported mothers, have to plan in relation to their own problems, hopes and fears. Parents who have actually lived with their children and who hope to be reunited sooner or later, usually have much to offer in large or small ways once they can be helped to appreciate themselves as parents.

George's work (1970) highlights the neglectful or even hostile attitude of some local authorities towards natural parents of children in foster-care. He quotes the belief of Keith-Lucas (1961) that 'those agencies which care most about the parent also care most about the child'. He mentions three reasons given by Glickman (1957, pp. 102-4) why parents should be prepared for their child's placement: first, to ameliorate the pain of separation both for parent and child; secondly, to maximise the chances of success of the placement by enlisting the natural parents' co-operation; thirdly, to prevent parents drifting away after the child's placement. Yet in George's study of preparations leading to the long-term placement of sixty children he found that, in the fifty-two cases where parents' addresses were known, there were only four cases where the parents were actively involved in the sense that workers arranged contacts between them and the foster-parents. As he says, social work literature is well aware of foster-parents' difficulties in meeting natural parents but it has under-emphasised the latter's difficulties in meeting foster-parents. George also studied 128 long-term placements (mentioned above in the foster-care section, chapter 4) and found that the attitudes of the three departments towards natural parents fell into five groups:

1. A general policy of *discouragement* of parents from contact with their children, varying from quiet exclusion of parents from the plans to active hostility: 40.6%
2. *Encouragement* of parents to maintain contact with or without possibility of family rehabilitation: 3.8%
3. A *passive* attitude of neither actively encouraging nor discouraging parents persistently—e.g. parents were allowed to visit the foster-home, but no attempts were made to find reasons for irregular visiting: 44.3%
4. *Inconsistent* attitudes—e.g. with a change of worker: 6.6%
5. *Other* attitudes—e.g. where the parent was dead/ seriously ill: 4.7%

George here again points up a discrepancy between theory

and practice, as it is generally agreed in the literature that parental visiting is desirable: first, in order to work towards family reunion (i.e. supposing that the parents are being helped to resolve their problems, and that their visits are a source of support to the children); secondly, even if reunion seems unlikely, parental visiting is considered conducive to the child's emotional health in that he tends otherwise to feel rejected, disloyal or to view his parents unrealistically. It is usually possible for workers to perceive the needs of parents and their children as complementary, not conflicting. George thinks the *passive* attitude listed above is slightly more hopeful for future practice, as it implies the willingness of workers to be more positive if they had more time.

Mapstone (1971) discusses ways of working with the parents of children in care. There is also Stevenson's paper (1968) about the meaning of reception into care for everybody concerned, including the worker; similarly chapter 7 in Timms (1962). The essence of their ideas can be summarised as the worker's responsibility to include the parents throughout the family upheaval—before, during and after the actual period of separation; and the worker's need to see beyond the apathy or sheer awkwardness of parents to their underlying grief, feelings of failure, expectations of criticism. Parents as well as children have fantasies, Mapstone says, sometimes reality-based and reinforced by newspaper headlines and television documentaries—fears of losing their children for ever, and of their children turning against them in favour of better substitute-parents. They tend to have strong views about the form of care selected: some find it more natural and homely to visit their child in foster-care; others feel less rivalry in meeting residential staff employed to look after children. If parents are out of sympathy with the plans, the child will be torn, and the arrangements more likely to break down. These ideas are applicable to a range of children, who may be committed under care orders, or in hospital or special boarding-schools for varying lengths of time.

First, parents must be included in the plans *before* their child leaves home—they may want to provide some clothes and toys, and to tell the worker special things about their child and his history. (If more children from the same family are leaving home than can be accommodated to-gether elsewhere, the parents may suggest which siblings will best partner each other.) Parents need to know what is likely to happen, to meet beforehand those who will be caring for the child and to arrange the pattern of future meetings. I once re-introduced two long-estranged sisters-in-law to each other, and then listened to their spontaneous discussion about the child who was to be fostered privately with her aunt while her mother had a major operation:

Mother: 'No, Doris, 'er ain't at all picky about 'er food ...'
Aunt: 'If 'er has a favourite toy or treasure, 'er must bring 'un ...'
Mother: 'Wally'll bring clean clothes by bread-van, Friday.'

The parent is heartened in considering how he can play a meaningful part in future, when he himself receives concern as an individual with difficulties. Overwhelmed parents sometimes write wildly abusive, threatening letters but presumably lack Bernstein's 'elaborated code' used by local authorities, which may reply in mystifying, politely hostile and manipulative phrases. It is perhaps idealistic to hope that the foster-mother may take the deprived parent under her wing as well as the child but, because many parents are envious of the care their child receives, it is helpful when caretakers can in small ways show regard for the parents as people who matter also. This reduces some of the pressure of discomfort but inevitably there is friction caused by mutual ambivalence. Visits are often difficult, and the foster-parents naturally feel critical if parents do not arrive on the expected day or come bolstered by drink, the current cohabitee or costly presents for the child, if parents are themselves critical over their child's welfare, fill him up with sweets and unrealistic promises, and depart leaving the caretakers exhausted and the child tearful, unsettled.

Sometimes the worker stands virtually alone in regarding such visits as worthwhile; spadework between visits is often necessary to help the two sets of parent-figures air their negative feelings and thus meet again more positively. Parents may be eased by reminders of better times in the past when they were more certain of their children's love. In the present they can be helped to give whatever they can to the situation in consistent small ways, rather than in making occasional extravagant gestures interspersed with months of silence. Depending partly on the generosity of the caretaker, a surprisingly constructive partnership may develop.

> One foster-mother was considerate enough to dress the baby in his own second-rate clothes for his mother's first visit instead of showing him off to perfection in his new Sunday best. Another foster-mother explained the difference she experienced in knowing natural parents as real people—earlier she had adopted a boy brought up from babyhood whose mentally-subnormal mother she never met; now she was having weekly visits from a young unmarried mother who expected someday to resume care herself: 'If I never see her, the baby feels like my own—when I know her, I know he belongs to her. I love them both, but not the same.'

This foster-mother expresses a basic reason why visits from natural parents are so necessary yet so difficult. But in so far as such visits limit the caretaker's emotional acceptance of a young child who is unlikely to return to his own parents, their value is debatable. It is foolish to pretend that every parent will respond positively to imaginative treatment; a few remain incorrigibly self-centred and changeable; some naturally enjoy an unaccustomed sense of power and cannot resist playing cat and mouse, especially when they see relationships strengthening within the substitute home. Workers are frequently torn between their belief in the importance of reuniting families and their belief that a child who is well-settled in a long-term substitute home should not be uprooted at the parents' whim. The only solutions to this dilemma lie first in positive prevention whenever possible of family breakdown; secondly in legal acknowledgment that when a child has merged into a safe foster-family where he feels to belong, his substitute home may truly have become his real home. Children can be invited to give an opinion on where they wish to live, but cannot take responsibility for a final decision.

The time factor is vital (as shown in the foster-care section in chapter 4) because it seems that many caretakers cannot tolerate prolonged uncertainty nor risk emotional involvement with children whom they may lose; yet, as time passes, children inevitably take root in a benign environment—these roots may gradually become stronger than neglected blood ties. Natural parents tend to deny this fact, along with their fears that their child may forget or dislike them once settled elsewhere—thus they may tend to forget him for indefinite periods and/or to reclaim him arbitrarily, as it is too difficult for them to consider his needs as distinct from their own. Mapstone (1971) suggests that parents should be helped appropriately to reclaim their children before a possessive foster-home situation develops. Workers may inevitably experience failure in 'educating' caretakers who have already enjoyed many years' undisputed possession of their foster-children, whereas prospective foster-parents can learn to some extent from the beginning to regard natural parents constructively.

George (1970, pp. 218-21) almost concludes that, once local authorities have provided the necessary services 'for the implementation of the parental role', then it is justifiable to test systematically the ability and willingness of parents to retain or resume care of their own children and, if necessary, to curtail their parental rights. To me, it seems both punitive and ineffective for a worker to strive for family reunion for a limited period and then, if the parents have not responded favourably, to declare them unfit. Such unfitness is hard to define legally or to prove consistently. However, when a young child has invested emotionally in his substitute home to the extent that his removal from safe caretakers would constitute serious bereavement for him, the actual qualities of his natural parents become less relevant—the vital question is not whether they are 'good' or 'bad' parents but where the child's needs will best be met. Legal denigration of parents, and legal reverence for parental rights, should become outmoded in favour of stronger emphasis on the child's own long-term well-being. In cases where it seems best for the child to be granted legal security within the foster-home, natural parents are unlikely to accept this solely for the child's sake but they can be helped to consider whether such a decision is also in their own best interests (see Malone, 1971).

The above three paragraphs do not contradict the hope that most parents with problems, given help, will have something to give their children. Here are some extracts from a verbatim record provided by Mary Wilkins. The worker is visiting Mrs Exe, whose eldest son, Anthony aged nine, is in residential care. Mr and Mrs Exe have three sons at home—two of school-age, and Toddy the youngest. After initial greetings, the worker is half-welcomed into the warm, chaotic kitchen:

Mrs Exe: 'Go out and play, Toddy ... stop grizzling. How am I supposed to know where your trousers are? Can't you see I'm talking? Get out ... I'm sick to death of it. I nearly went last Sunday. I don't care—they can all be put away.'

S W: 'You're feeling pretty bad?'

Mrs Exe: 'I'm feeling bloody awful ... (*she enlarges about shortage of money and her hatred of everybody, especially her husband*) ... I'll go, and that'll give him something to grumble about. The lads won't care—they don't want me ...'

S W gradually conveys that Anthony is wanting to see her

Mrs Exe: 'I'm not visiting him. What good will that do? You took him away from me at that Court, you can get on with it. I'm not going to see him if he doesn't want me.'

S W: 'You are worried about seeing him—'

Mrs Exe: 'Of course I'm not. All I'm worried about is that he might not want to see me.'

S W: 'Oh, I see.'

Mrs Exe: 'He doesn't think much of me ... (*elaborates, and suggests that Anthony prefers the worker visiting instead, and anyway she herself has nothing material to give him*) ... Toddy, go out and play again. He's always on about something—'

S W: '... I was saying that giving things doesn't matter much.'

Mrs Exe: 'I know, I heard you. You don't understand ... I feel awful when I go there. I know you think I'm hard, but I just can't go. I'm afraid he'll say something.'

S W: 'Say something?'

Mrs Exe: 'He's always saying he likes his father better than me—I've always done all I can ... made no difference. He was a terrible baby, always crying ... sometimes I couldn't stop him crying and I felt as though I'd do something dreadful.'

S W: 'Yes, you did have a bad time, didn't you?'

Mrs Exe: 'Bad time? Nobody knows what I had to put up with. Nobody cared ... Nobody cares now ... (*elaborates on her miserable childhood and early married life*) ... so I don't see why I should be expected to do everything for Anthony. I bet you think I'm awful—'

S W: 'You have been under a lot of pressure.'

137

Mrs Exe: (*continues about her husband*) '... I can't stand him now. Anthony was born straightaway. I used to look at him sometimes and think he might die ... He didn't know I was thinking that about him.'

S W: 'Anthony is very fond of you. He told me how you used to read him stories when he was little. He liked that and he remembered it.'

Mrs Exe: '... Yes, I did. Somehow he wasn't so bad. I used to wallop him sometimes—I suppose he has told you—'

S W: 'He talks mostly about the good times at home ...'

Mrs Exe: 'It's funny he remembers good things—what does he say? (*They continue backwards and forwards over the same ground for some time*) ... I'm fed up with everything. I shall go and leave the lot. Fancy Anthony remembering about picnics and that ...'

S W: 'That was a good side.'

Mrs Exe: 'Don't be silly. Want a cup of tea? (*makes it, but returns without it*) ... I can't visit him, not if you went on your bended knees—too difficult ... buses don't fit in ...'

S W: 'I think you're afraid of the feelings it might stir up.'

Mrs Exe: 'What? His feelings? He doesn't care.'

S W: 'No, your feelings—you probably feel mixed up in your feelings about him.'

Mrs Exe: 'You do keep on, don't you? (*gradually fetches the tea, begins to consider visiting Anthony, wanting to discuss her feelings again and to know the worker's picture of her as a mother, repeats former doubts, screams to Toddy to come indoors immediately*) ... I shall go on Saturday to see Anthony. If he wants to see me, of course ... Toddy can come with me.'

That conversation happened to be with a mother whose eldest son was separated from her—its gist might equally well have been with any parent-figure in difficulties over a child at home, even with an exasperated caretaker demanding to be relieved of her charge. (Unfortunately mothers have figured more than fathers in this chapter's case-examples, which serves to emphasise our frequent neglect of father-figures requiring similar help.)

The emphasis throughout both sections of this chapter is on accepting openly the immediate emotional pressures of parent-figures in order to help them to meet the emotional needs of children dependent upon them. Therefore it is important to finish with *the third stage* of helping a reunited family to settle down again, and of helping caretakers to relinquish children to whom they have grown attached. Discussion of separation and of testing-out the new environment usually centres on the original parting, but a child's return home after any length of time involves a second upheaval for all concerned and a renewed testing-out by the child. When Anthony returns home, Mrs Exe will need considerable support if she is to tolerate the inevitable testing by him of her affection. Similarly, discussion of separation usually centres on the child's reaction; more thought is required about its effects on the parents.

Kay (1970) studied the impact of compulsory removal of children on family cohesion, and found a high incidence of subsequent breakdown of the parents' marriage. Jeans (1969) describes how families stagnated in their grief-reactions long after the removal of a mentally subnormal member to hospital. Holtom (1968) believes that workers should 'keep the sense of loss alive' by presenting a realistic picture of the missing child to the family which has excluded him. S. Jenkins (1969) contributed to Fanshel's study (1971, mentioned in the foster-care section, chapter 4) by interviewing separately a large number of natural parents of New York City foster-children to find what feelings these parents had experienced at the time of separation.

Sadness at the time of parting was the feeling Jenkins found most commonly reported; other feelings (in decreasing order) were worry, nervousness, anger, bitterness, thankfulness and relief. Next in order was guilt (more in mothers) and shame (more in fathers); feelings of numbness and paralysis were least reported. Mothers in relatively high socio-economic circumstances were significantly more thankful and relieved upon placement; thankfulness was also linked with a face-saving reason for placement such as the mother's physical illness. Mothers in lower socio-economic circumstances were more nervous and worried on the day their children entered foster-care; nervousness over placement was also linked with parents' authoritarian child-rearing attitudes. Analysis of the length of time for which children remained in care showed that feelings of anger, bitterness and worry were significantly associated with those cases where children were discharged from care in less than one year.

This suggests that parents' feelings and attitudes at the time of placement may be predictive of its outcome. Does the anger Jenkins describes suggest a potentiality to fight constructively for their children's return, in contrast to parents who internalise negative feelings and tend to accept the placement passively? Westheimer (1970) as a by-product of her work with Heinicke (1965), presents evidence that waning of the maternal response occurs during separation and that the length of separation is an important factor.

'Intimate communication between mother and child is dependent upon their togetherness and diminishes during separation.' Parallel with the three observable phases of protest, despair and detachment in the young child? 'That the child is being cared for by others frequently affects a mother's estimation of her own importance to her child. Prior to the event of reunion, all the mothers experienced apprehension ... half the mothers in the sample delayed the return of their child for inadequate reasons' (e.g. house-decorating); some of these mothers of young children remained detached in their attitude to the child even after reunion following more lengthy separation (e.g. went out to work, leaving others to daily-mind).

It is unfortunate and uneconomic when hard-pressed social workers leave parents to deal in ignorance with the aftermath of reunion, because relationships deteriorate further if the parents react with hostility to their child's initial unsettlement. Caretakers may also be left stranded without recognition that the actual parting, even when long-anticipated, is painful and leaves questions such as, 'Did it unsettle him, to get fond of us and then go home, as much as it has upset me? Was it all worth it—for him? for me? Do I ever want to get involved like that again?' The worker may visit weeks later, wanting urgently to discuss the next placement, but reluctantly has to spend an hour first discussing the previous child. Caretakers, having lived with a child, are less able than fieldworkers to move on to the next assignment, and it is in the interests of subsequent children if they can be helped to recover self-confidence in between.

6

Other ways of helping children

Their coming together now, after two years of married life, was much more wonderful to them than it had been before ... Anna's soul was put at peace between them. She looked from one to the other, and she saw them established to her safety, and she was free. She played between the pillar of fire and the pillar of cloud in confidence, having the assurance on her right hand and the assurance on her left. She was no longer called upon to uphold with her childish might the broken end of the arch. Her father and her mother now met to the span of the heavens, and she, the child, was free to play in the space beneath, between.

(D. H. Lawrence: *The Rainbow*)

As a child Dickens experienced that initial irritation of spirit and deprivation which can frequently be the source of either neurosis and criminality, or of a passionate but valid social criticism ... The child became for him the symbol of sensitive feelings anywhere in a society maddened with the pursuit of material progress.

(Peter Coveney: *The Image of Childhood*)

This final chapter considers briefly other ways of helping children. The happy state of affairs in Anna's family is what one would wish ideally for any child. It was achieved without social work help—which recalls an early suggestion that potentiality for development lies within people themselves. Yet Anna's background was complex: the marriage described above was between her immigrant Polish mother and an English step-father; her own father had died when she was a year old—she was fiercely possessive of her mother and, aged four, initially resentful of her mother's second marriage. Lawrence describes (chapters 2, 3) how Anna and her step-father became close, and how the man only narrowly escaped battering Anna's resistance to him while his wife was in labour.

Suppose Anna's family had required social work intervention: my own inclination would be to offer casework help to the step-father (or to the mother if she seemed more aware of having problems), but there would be several ways of attempting to ease the situation, depending largely on what the family itself wished and on what the worker had to offer. In other words, Anna's soul might have gained a measure of peace, freedom and confidence through joining a play group, through the influence of a behaviour therapist, through joint discussion within the family group or within a group of worried parents ... Whatever the method(s) chosen, the aim would be much the same, so there is room for flexibility according to circumstance, except it is rarely true that the end justifies the means. Bartlett (1970) makes an original contribution towards a coherent picture of social work interventions; or Tilbury (1971) discusses briefly some criteria in the selection of casework, group work and community work methods. The study of the Canford Families (ed. Howarth, 1962) records an early attempt to assess the value of family casework alongside children's groups. My second quotation about Dickens sets the scene for a final word in this chapter about social concern for children in their families.

Behaviour therapy

Relevant literature includes Laycock (1970, pp. 83-9, 101-2) who sees value in assessment and treatment which is informed, though not dominated, by learning theory principles; Jehu's clear exposition (1967) of learning theory and social work—also his article (1968) about the treatment of childhood phobias in residential settings. Beech (1969) presents a good discussion of ways of changing man's behaviour, and Ullman and Krasner (1965) devote a section of thirteen papers to deviant behaviour in children—e.g. the elimination of tantrum behaviour by extinction procedures; effects of social reinforcement on isolate behaviour of a nursery school-child; shaping adaptive behaviour in a therapeutic summer camp. Picardie (1969) writes on learning, communication and 'games'. Beech (p. 17) says the behaviour therapist is orientated towards removing the patient's symptoms by allowing the patient to unlearn maladaptive behaviour or to learn some new piece of adaptive behaviour. Jehu (1967, chapter 4) deals with methods of child-training, including discussion of feeding, crying, dependency and punishment—e.g.:

(p. 51) 'Feeding problems can be established and modified by reinforcement. The child who refuses to eat, may be being positively reinforced for not doing so by parental fussing, coaxing and attention. If a child is punished for not eating, food may acquire secondary negative reinforcing qualities so that it will be avoided ... just as the punishment itself is.' And (p. 52) 'For most parents, an infant's cries are noxious stimuli which elicit caretaking activities' ... Crying may be 'forestalled by anticipating stresses and removing them ... (or by) reinforcing behaviour which the child may use instead of crying, such as verbal requests. Finally, crying may be extinguished by not reinforcing it.' And (p. 68) 'As a disciplinary technique, reasoning seems to have some advantages over physical punishment ... Alternative methods of socialization to punishment, which do not involve its disadvantages, include positive reinforcement of desired behaviour and extinction.'

Some of this seems common sense, though worth comparing with Woodmansey's belief (1966 b) that a child who is confident that his parents will come when he calls in the night will not call unless he needs them:

This is not, of course, a plea for giving a child everything he asks for; though there seems to be no point in refusing a child's request for the sake of some disciplinary principle. There are occasions when the parent must make unwelcome decisions; and it is then the child that was freely gratified as a baby, and is now on friendly terms with his parents, that will most readily accept the consequent disappointment.

He also shows the illogicality of slapping children to 'teach' them to avoid danger, and particularly of the mother who bites her child in order to teach him not to bite— 'despite her own immediate experience that on her it has had just the opposite effect ... But is this attitude really different from that of the many people (including psychiatrists and social workers) who seem unable to accept that true morality depends, not on fear of punishment, but on friendly feelings and positive identifications?'

Possibly social workers are increasingly aware that punishment is destructive (and indeed is only effective at the cost of personality damage) but many would agree with behaviour therapists that it is quite acceptable to use 'positive reinforcers' (i.e. rewards, praise) instead of 'negative reinforcers' (i.e. punishment, blame). This may be so, though it should be understood that emphasis on reward and praise implies the possibility of punishment and blame, and that 'the withdrawal of positive reinforcers' (i.e. withholding pocket money, treats, approval, love) is a euphemism for punishment. However, caseworkers and behaviour therapists share more educational ground than is commonly recognised and, rather than enter further into any controversy (on which Kay, 1969, gives a comparatively balanced viewpoint), I prefer to indicate three areas where learning theory might prove unequivocally useful.

These areas are the habit-training of severely subnormal children; intervention in prolonged crisis-states; and the treatment of some school-refusal problems. First, it would seem that the use of behaviour therapy techniques in helping to socialise severely subnormal children can be justified on the grounds that such children, given more attractive and convenient habits, will become less burdensome and therefore on better terms with their parents or caretakers. Beech (1969) and Ullmann and Krasner (1965) describe methods involving positive incentives and the ignoring of undesirable behaviour. The danger is that these children could conceivably be used as subjects for experiments which would not be sanctioned for 'normal' children.

Secondly, when intervening in prolonged crisis-situations, social workers might consider whether they sometimes encourage clients to be chaotic. A crisis is usually, by definition, a temporary state, when people are accessible to social work help, but multi-problem families and disturbed adolescents may experience (and cause) prolonged crisis. Even those workers who repudiate behaviour therapy are more influenced by learning theory than they know, and could usefully recognise this. Clients sometimes forget to say when their situation has eased, perhaps fearing we are only interested in trouble. Foster-parents may find they can gain essential attention only by producing a major crisis, by which time it may be too late to avoid the foster-children's removal. Multi-problem families have little outlet for entertainment: crises may be their best way to break the drab monotony, and the worker may be invited to attend an evening's marital drama though it is possibly more effective for him to visit next day. These examples are arguments for giving attention in between crises, for helping multi-problem families to verbalise the meaning and pattern of critical events (see Hill, 1965), for demonstrating a reaction to problems which families may learn to imitate, for defining an end to crises, for meeting clients in fair weather as well as foul, which may mean literally going for a picnic with them instead of awaiting the next emergency call. Similarly, disturbed adolescents are time-consuming, and some time spent ahead of potential crises could reduce the time devoted to mopping-up operations—for example:

> Sue, aged 5, was placed in County A with foster-parents who soon moved to County B. When Sue was 16 years old, the foster-home broke down. County B hoped County A would now resume direct responsibility for this difficult girl. Both counties might have argued lengthily over their respective duties, making Sue feel unwanted in either place. However, County A invited her and her worker from County B to spend a day in her former area, where Sue was welcomed, taken to see places she knew as a little girl and to meet people who remembered her pleasantly. Sue decided she would like to find residential employment in County A, going back to her foster-parents for occasional weekends. Subsequently she was still difficult, but perhaps more trusting than she would have been otherwise.

Thirdly, behaviour therapy techniques may be useful in treating school-phobia. This is a difficult problem for all concerned, including the worker who is usually under great pressure to return the child quickly to school. He easily reinforces the child's distress by making unsuccessful attempts to hasten return to school; then pressure mounts over a period of months while the child grows more fearful and the adults more helpless, culminating drastically perhaps in the child's compulsory removal from home. Most of this could be avoided if a first step was to ease the pressure by obtaining medical permission for the child to stay away from school for a time while the situation was assessed. Caseworkers would tend to look for conflicts in relationships at home or at school; learning theorists would seek ways of re-introducing the child into a habit of attending school. Perhaps a combination of these methods is appropriate, as the child may displace some of his fears on to school even though the problem stems from family relationships. Kahn and Nursten (1968) discuss thoroughly the treatment of school-refusal as a psycho-social problem, and include a mention of behaviour therapy (p. 209). Jehu (1967) quotes examples of systematic desensitisation to school-phobia :

> Social workers shared in the treatment of a group of children for school-phobia, in which affection, reassurance, approval and friendliness, were provided to evoke pleasant emotional responses during a series of graded tasks, starting with the mother sitting in the classroom with the child and going on to his helping in the school office, sitting near a friend, and finally remaining in school for gradually increasing periods of time. (p. 89, from Talbot, 1957.)

A less pleasant example (Eysenck and Rachman, 1965, via Jehu, p. 86) is of a thirteen-year-old boy, Leslie, who was 'desensitised to a hierarchy commencing with playing in the school grounds and terminating with being struck by a master in the classroom'.

This climax is perhaps not so much an argument against behaviour therapy as an indictment of the punitive conditions at school which required Leslie's grooming for being hit. At the end of treatment he was attending school normally—one wonders how enjoyably, and how sympathetic he will be towards his own children some day. Beech (1969, chapter 4) describes similarly the building of anxiety hierarchies in which either real or imaginary situations are used. An appropriate programme, or hierarchy, is devised, starting with situations involving least anxiety and progressing steadily to those involving most. The worker has also to decide upon the form of the anxiety-inhibiting response which he wishes the patient to use in the presence of the usual cues for anxiety.

To sum up, there would seem to be practical value in a caseworker planning the child's return to school in easy stages. An early stage might well be the use of a specially selected home-teacher who could give pleasant individual attention to the child and support to the whole family. The school itself should participate (see Kahn and Nursten, 1968, p. 215) and teachers may need help in modifying their attitudes towards troubled children. Simple truancy is not a serious problem and is best not reinforced by treating it as such.

Group work and community work

This section consists largely of references to recorded experiments in group work of which several examples are given in recent journals. These papers show that successful groups do not happen by spontaneous combustion: there is considerable thought behind the scenes at every stage, particularly in planning beforehand the purpose and composition of groups. Workers may start by drawing upon theory relevant to their immediate needs, and then re-think when theory becomes meaningful in practice. McCullough and Ely (1968) introduce a range of theory and practice in social group work, and Douglas (1970) reviews small group theory in the last decade. Similarly, Richardson (1967) introduces group study for teachers. The Central Training Council in Child Care compiled studies in field-work training (HMSO, 1971) with sections on play-groups, group and community work placements, recording the ideas of students, supervisors and tutors.

In the study of the Canford families (ed. Howarth, 1962)

it was found beneficial for an experimental agency to offer direct help to children in groups as well as casework help to their parents. Hamilton (chapter VI) and Laufer (chapter VII) convey in vivid detail their groups' interaction, and show how the experience, especially of identification with the leader, can help children to cope more easily with tensions arising at home or at school. Roseman and Cooke (1964) give another early account of social group work with children in family casework agency; the aim was defined as 'helping people to develop and use their capacities for satisfying social relationships and for making constructive use of the resources in their environment'. They found that the groups went through three stages: first, a period of familiarising themselves with the setting; followed by a period of acting-out when the leader's influence was important; thirdly, a period of constructive play gradually emerged with greater social participation, more self-assurance and better mastery of play materials.

Groups for young children usually revolve round play; those for older people may be activity-based or for discussion of problems and experience shared in common. L. Walker (1970), with an introduction by Irvine, describes her group of F S U mothers who became less inarticulate and more self-confident; Bond (1969) writes of an F S U fathers' group which unexpectedly turned itself into a playgroup. Recent accounts particularly worth reading are those of L. Walker, Davies (1966), Tyndale and Porter (1971) and contributors to Tod's collected papers. Tyndale and Porter evaluate their experience of play therapy groups for asthmatic children alongside discussion groups for the parents to help them accept change in their children; Lavan (1970) also describes simultaneous groups in a psychiatric setting, and Henderson & Leach (1971) an experimental group for adolescents as a form of preventive work.

Anthony (1968) discusses group therapy techniques in residential units; he conducted groups for children, for their parents, for the staff—and for groups of staff and children together, which may be slightly akin to conjoint family therapy. Pollack (1971) describes 'a sensitivity training (or T-group) approach to group therapy with children', which in fact sounds somewhat insensitive: the first learning task of a small, closed group of variously-disturbed children is 'to grasp the get-give ratio' (i.e. that what they receive from the world is directly related to their willingness to give) through confrontation with the leader. The children's behaviour was mirrored in the leader's response —e.g. to a hostile child, 'Your behaviour is upsetting me, I'm getting angry at you'. Two-thirds of the children were said, by school reports, to have improved as a result of the 6-8 weeks' course; the withdrawn children responded quickly, while the extremely hostile, hyperactive children had the poorest prognosis. Group dynamics have destructive as well as constructive potentials.

Papers about social work in adoption (ed. Tod, 1971 a) include Dillow on the group process in adoptive home-finding, McWhinnie on group counselling with seventy-eight adoptive families, and Sandgrund on group counselling after legal adoption. Running parallel are papers about social work in foster-care (ed. Tod, 1971 b), including Stanley on an excellent group method of recruiting, selecting and preparing foster-parents; Ball and Bailey on group work with experienced foster-parents, Watson and Boverman on pre-adolescent foster-children in group discussions, and Carter on groups of adolescent foster-children. The pre-adolescent members usually began by denying their difference from other children but, with support, showed an urgent desire to understand their circumstances; they also became more active in seeking the help of their individual caseworkers outside the group. The leaders saw their role as finding but not treating problems; they had 'to guard against the temptation to treat the children as the children's anxiety mounted'. It is debatable whether children should be expected to contain newly-disclosed problems, but the justification here was the caseworkers' availability to individual children in between group sessions. Clearly some pattern must be worked out between preserving confidentiality within the group and ensuring co-ordination between group workers and caseworkers.

Group work overlaps with community work, and references here to the latter overlap with the final section on social concern. Smith (1970 a) discusses short-term foster-parents as a form of community worker, and (1970 b) seeks resolution of conflict between the social worker's role as a caseworker and his wider responsibility in social reform. A report on youth and community work in the seventies (H M S O, 1969) proposes a service more geared to the needs of young people participating within the community and away from the club-based approach, with work among the younger age groups becoming mainly the responsibility of schools and voluntary organisations. Craft, Raynor and Cohen (1967) edit papers with a sociological approach to linking home, school and community. Lady Allen of Hurtwood (1968), still campaigning for children, describes creative experiments in community planning for children's play in several countries. Holme and Massie (1970) report on three separate pieces of research in their study of children's play related to environmental facilities; they discuss the concept of play provision as a social service, showing the need for a local authority policy on play facilities, which should be imaginatively designed and diversely suitable for all ages and weathers.

Conjoint family therapy

This has been defined (via Milloy, 1971) as 'the process of planned intervention in an area of family dysfunctioning. It is centred on the dynamic function of the family as a unit, and some form of multiple interviewing is the primary treatment technique.' Relevant literature includes Ackerman (1966), Satir (1967), and articles by Laing (1969), Goldberg (1968), Schneider (1969) and Skynner (1971). In family therapy, the casework focus is shifted from the individual's problem to the context of inter-personal relationships within the family group. The family members may cover two or three generations with a wide range of age and strength; all have vulnerabilities in relation to each other—particularly perhaps the children. This is unlike social group work, where members tend to be of the same generation, without blood ties, able to support each other to some extent through sharing some interest or handicap in common.

A social worker requires skill in order to adapt his methods to the individual needs of people in a particular situation; he also needs to know which methods he personally finds most comfortable and to develop an individual style which suits his clients. The idea of conjoint family therapy has been received with varying degrees of enthusiasm in this country; few workers so far have planned its deliberate use (though it may happen accidentally on a home visit); many caseworkers have a healthy doubt of their ability to handle a session where emotional sparks are likely to flare painfully round the family circle. Such a session may have diagnostic value in that the worker experiences family interaction at first hand, though I doubt the extent to which effective treatment is possible. Laing's paper (1969) emphasises the value of studying a situation with the whole family in its own home rather than assuming that any individual member can present an objective picture. Workers accept that clients usually speak truly from their own subjective viewpoint, but it is alarming to consider how often this is recorded and acted upon as factual evidence.

Goldberg's paper (1968) is useful in presenting factors requiring consideration in family diagnosis but, as an alternative here, I will borrow some questions which Barbara

Butler suggests the worker might ask himself:

1. Who or what is presented as the problem in this family? Who or what is having to carry the complaints of the family?
2. How has this family group managed its problems before —what is different now? e.g. the parents might have coped when the children were small, but cannot now send adolescents out to play—or perhaps a previously helpful grandmother has died.
3. How does the family compare with its particular cultural norm? What are the expectations of the neighbourhood group on this family and vice versa?
4. What kind of interior family environment do they have and how do they use their available space? How do they eat, sleep, play ...?
5. How do they communicate—with words, gestures, blows, food, through a child or through the dog ...? Do members themselves feel they communicate satisfyingly?
6. Who is the key person (whose co-operation is required if the worker is to be effective)?
7. What kind of family pattern does there tend to be? e.g. scapegoating, pairing, adhesive, disorganised.

These patterns are commented on briefly below, from my own viewpoint.

Scapegoating is one of the most typical patterns in a dysfunctional family, where one member (often a child) acts out the family conflict projected on to him. The emotional well-being of the chosen person (sometimes known as the elected or identified patient) is sacrificed to maintain the balance (or homeostasis) of the family. Those in favour of conjoint family therapy believe that, by meeting as a group, this kind of family can be helped together to see what is happening, and each member can be helped to accept his share of the badness. But it is painfully difficult to withdraw a projection, and one could argue that help is best offered privately to a key member.

Pairing (e.g. of a parent-child or husband-wife) exists where one couple's relationship is exclusively important within the family, causing a warped pattern throughout. Presumably the therapist would seek to re-introduce members of the family circle to each other on a more realistic basis. Satir (1967, part I) discusses the interaction in a marriage where both partners have low self-esteem; the partners grow disillusioned though still dependent on each other, looking to their child for reassurance.

The adhesive family is perhaps more typical of 'nice' middle-class families, where all is rosy, with no cross words, no secrets, few individual outlets—until one member breaks out, or breaks down in health. The plan in conjoint family therapy would be to help them to express some of the hidden resentment and, hopefully, for them to discover they are not destroyed as a family through recognising natural ambivalence.

The disorganised family has lost its positive feelings just as the adhesive family has lost touch with its negative feelings. Conjoint therapy is less practicable here as members rarely congregate, and the parents' unmet needs would probably dominate the group.

Clearly such therapy is inappropriate in cases where the family is very disorganised, where communication has quite broken down, where there is a very paranoid person/ a rigidly defended person/a person dominated by unmet needs/a disturbed person needing individual treatment. It appears that a family requires some measure of strength and willingness to communicate before such help can be offered; naturally it will only slowly realise that the worker does not take sides or allocate blame. Exponents of the method claim special value in working with the family group in *a crisis-situation*: the value here lies in learning how the critical event is perceived by various members; in avoiding an expedient solution at the expense of one member, in supporting and steering the group towards more effective future coping-patterns.

Ackerman (1966) and others attempt 'to activate the dormant interpersonal conflicts into the here and now of family interaction', thus making them accessible to solution. Abbreviated here is Ackerman's summary of the therapist's functions (pp. 100-1): he establishes empathy and communication within the family; he clarifies conflict by dissolving barriers, disguises and misunderstandings; he is in part a parent figure controlling danger and giving warm support; he works through resistances by the use of confrontation and interpretation; he educates, challenges, reintegrates. The worker simultaneously stirs up trouble and controls its expression. Ackerman's chapter 5 bristles with active (? attacking) verbs—the therapist pierces, tickles the defences, activates a shift, shakes-up pre-existing alignments, breaks down anxiety-ridden taboos, uses a method that hits home ... I visualise Ackerman himself as a benign bull in a china shop—but is there some danger of a family becoming so alarmed, angry and humiliated that it feels it might as well go the whole hog and then wallows in mud-slinging without feeling very much at all? A serious flaw in the method seems to be the difficulty of responding helpfully and simultaneously to the conflicting needs of two generations (unlike the 'peer group' situation characteristic of social group work).

Family therapists argue that it is preferable for children to hear straight out what is wrong, rather than be uneasy through unexpressed family conflicts. Is there special value in 'having everything out in the open' unless an individual's negative feelings can be received in terms of their specific effect on him, and how can the worker empathise with a parent's painful anger about a child when the child is actually listening? It is doubtful, in one of Ackerman's examples, whether John aged 16 and Peg aged 11 appreciate hearing (throughout pp. 8-20) of their mother's habit of belching into their father's face in bed. Nor is the parents' dignity enhanced in their own eyes in this session. Children typically interrupt, plead headaches, change the subject, try to leave the room, when the topic becomes too dangerous; the therapist interprets their evasiveness and attempts to show that parental quarrels are tolerable— e.g. (Satir, 1967, p. 150): 'I think both children get upset when their mother and father disagree. Maybe they think someone will get hurt. But I don't see any dead bodies around, do you?' Presumably foster-children would be particularly vulnerable if foster-family therapy were to become fashionable.

Satir's method, outlined step by step in her book, is less complex, though still very controlling: a way of teaching family members to perceive their roles and relationships more realistically and to communicate more successfully. She includes two useful chapters on communication theory, and does not allow any member to voice another's opinion or emotion—'When you speak, speak for yourself only'. Questions are put to each member in turn, with a feedback on their verbal and non-verbal replies. She takes a joint family history which may clear misunderstandings and enable children to imagine their parents as individuals and partners before they were born. She also gives a view of the family as the child sees it; his perception of the way his parents treat each other and himself. The book contains suggestions for what the worker may say if the situation gets out of hand (p. 166)—the most drastic being, 'When you can talk in an adult manner, then come back and we'll get to work. Until then we will have to terminate therapy.'

To sum up, conjoint family therapy is available as a method; we can decide whether or not to accept it in whole or in part. It is clearly useful sometimes to make a deliberate effort to see the whole family together: perhaps for a diagnostic enquiry under the 1969 Act, and in crisis-situations. Sometimes a worker may visit and find himself with the entire family, either by accident or by the family's design, and some understanding of family therapy would help the worker to use this unexpected situation positively. British families are perhaps unlikely to show great enthusiasm for such therapy, but they may on occasion like the idea of 'family meetings' for discussing plans and ideas:

> An NSPCC worker (who may not have heard of conjoint family therapy at that time) introduced family committee meetings in one case. The father had been left with eight children aged from 19 to 4 when his wife died; he continued his own role of breadwinner and expected the eldest girls in turn to keep house. After the first daughter married and the second was in charge, the third girl saw the pattern and became pregnant in her own right, aged 15. At this point the family welcomed and took very seriously the worker's suggestion of family committee meetings. Normally they were unable to discuss things on their own. The worker was chairman, but deferred to the father, heard each member's viewpoint and tried to reach joint decisions. The family gradually became more self-supporting.

Social concern

In a study (ed. Holman, 1970) of socially deprived families in Britain, Lafitte estimates that, in 1966, 365,000 families (containing 995,000 children) were in poverty by the old assistance standard, and 450,000 families (containing 1,215,000 children) were in poverty by the new standard. Another contributor, Spencer, shows that low income earners are much more likely to live in unfit accommodation, and Wilson highlights inadequacies in the field of child socialisation—e.g. the link between low income and educational deprivation. Holman, summing up the whole, stresses that social deprivation is frequently multiple in nature; he lists groups which are deprived in terms of income, housing and child socialisation: low wage earners, large families, fatherless families (see Wynn, 1964, 1970), the unemployed, the sick and disabled, immigrants, tinkers and caravan-dwellers.

Holman sees a tendency for deprived families to be concentrated in particular and definable areas, which implies that such areas could receive priority in terms of positive discrimination. (Coates and Silburn, 1970, describe the nature of poverty amongst the people of St Ann's, Nottingham and, in chapter 6, the effect on the children's development. Rex and Moore, 1967, studied a twilight zone of Birmingham which was perpetuated by a policy of discrimination creating avoidable racial tensions.) Having looked at gaps in the poverty provision and at possible reasons why the socially deprived fail to take up services and benefits designed to help them, Holman considers the present lack of client participation, the growth of client organisations (such as Mothers in Action) and pressure groups (such as C P A G, Shelter) and the pros and cons of militancy. He emphasises the role of social research in identifying deprivation (with the help of fieldworkers), in developing measurement tools and advising on forms of help.

Schreiber (1971) reports on the H E L P line for parents in Hollywood: this was set up as a demonstration project for three months in summer 1969 with the co-operation of schools and hospitals. The response was over 500 telephone calls, apparently many from 'hard to reach' families seeking help through a different kind of service; the greatest number of requests stemmed from concern about adolescent children. Leissner (1967), studying family advice services in this country, gained the impression that most F A S clients come from the lower socio-economic groups and that the predominant problems were those involving child-rearing, marital conflict, debts, housing. Leissner visited a representative sample of sixteen local authority departments, most of which had established an advisory service in some form, linked with statutory or voluntary agencies, though the key concepts of 'prevention' and 'advice' had not been uniformly or clearly defined. Other studies emanating from the National Children's Bureau have been mentioned earlier, and show a new breadth of concern for children in general. A preventive approach has been emphasised throughout this book, especially in relation to those caring for children.

Three addresses:

National Children's Bureau—
    Director: Dr M. L. Kellmer Pringle,
      Adam House, 1 Fitzroy Square, London W 1

Mothers in Action—
    25 Milton Road, London N 6

Child Poverty Action Group—
    1 Macklin Street, London W C 2

Suggestions for further reading

Possibly the preceding six chapters contain a surfeit of references—therefore only few further books are introduced here; the main emphasis is on re-grouping some earlier suggestions.

First, there are three companion volumes of immediate relevance in the L S W series: *Social Work in Child Care* (Pugh, 1968) which describes clearly the central tasks of local authority departments; *Residential Life with Children* (Beedell, 1970), and *Adolescence and Social Work* (Laycock, 1970).

Secondly, constant reference has been made to books of collected papers—especially to those of Clare Winnicott (1964), some of whose phrases are known by heart in child care circles; Robert Tod (1968 a & b, 1971 a & b) and Mrs Dockar Drysdale (1968)—all these contain excellent papers on social work with children. Longmans may publish a further selection on *communication with children*. Other collections relate to play in child care (*R C C A Review*, 1967), social work with families (ed. Younghusband, 1965), crisis theory (ed. Parad, 1965), and child socialisation from a sociological viewpoint (ed. Danziger, 1970).

Thirdly, child rearing studies: the Newsons (1963, 1968) give vivid impressions of Nottingham mothers' experience; there is also Wilson's concise section (ed. Holman, 1970) on the socialisation of children; J. Klein's *Samples from*

English Cultures (vol. 2, 1965); the classic work of Sears, Maccoby & Levin (1957); and Yarrow, Campbell & Burton (1968) enquire into child-rearing research and methods.

Fourthly, research: Bowlby's Penguin (1953, 2nd edition 1965) is an abridged version of his original monograph (1951); the second edition contains an additional section by Ainsworth, on further research into the adverse effects of maternal deprivation. Bowlby's recent work comprises two volumes—on *Attachment* (1969), and on *Loss*. Packman (1968) shows the diversity of child care policy and practice within this country. George (1970) reviews theory and practice in foster-care alongside his findings in three local authority departments. Neel's paper (1971) considers 'American trends and dilemmas in child welfare research'. A steady stream of studies flows from the National Children's Bureau (listed in the bibliography under Pringle, Dinnage, Parfit, Leissner etc.)—these have great value in their concern with the whole child, whether 'normal' or handicapped, their reviews of research and the multi-disciplinary, preventive approach.

Fifthly, historical accounts of child care: Heywood (1959) describes the development of the service for deprived children from the seventeenth century to the mid-twentieth century; Hopkirk (1949) tells the story of the unwelcomed child from 1530-1948; Middleton (1971) evaluates substitute care provided in the first half of this century. George (1970, chapter 1) studies foster-care in the nineteenth century; Pugh (1968, chapters 1 and 2) presents briefly the background to the 1948 and 1963 Acts; Boss (1971) explores developments in the child care service during the twenty years between Curtis and Seebohm. Ellison (1958, chapter 2) gives a brief history of adoption; Carlbach (1970) of the treatment of delinquent children; and Balbernie (1966) of disturbed and deprived children. In a wider context than all the foregoing, Pinchbeck and Hewitt (1969, vol. 1) survey children in English society from Tudor times to the eighteenth century; volume 2 will continue to the mid-twentieth century.

An autobiographical account of her childhood in care is given by Mrs Janet Hitchman (1960); Pugh (1968) lists three others in her bibliography. Lastly, a general favourite is Axline's true story of Dibs (1966); she has also written *Play Therapy: the inner dynamics of childhood* (1947). Rogers (1965) contains a chapter on play therapy, and Dr D. W. Winnicott's recently published work (1971) is on *Playing and Reality*.

Bibliography

ABBATT, P. (1967) 'Toys and play', *Play in Child Care*, R C C A Review, Vol. 15.

A C C O (1969), Monograph No. 3, *Adoption—The Way Ahead*, Davies, J. *et al.*: Assoc. Child Care Officers.

ACKERMAN, N. (1966) *Treating the Troubled Family*, New York/ London: Basic Books.

ADAMSON, G. (1969) 'How children's depts. treat their foster parents', *Case Conference*, Vol. 15, No. 10, Feb.

AINSWORTH, M. *et al.* (1962) *Deprivation of Maternal Care—a re-assessment of its effects*, Geneva: World Health Organisa- tion. (1965) in part III, 2nd edition, *Child Care & the Growth of Love*, J. Bowlby.

ALLEN OF HURTWOOD, LADY (1968) *Planning for Play*, London: Thames & Hudson.

ANCONA, L. (1970) 'An experimental contribution to the problem of identification with the father', in *Readings in Child Socialization*, ed. K. Danziger.

ANDREWS, R. (1971) 'When is subsidized adoption preferable to long-term foster care?', *J. Child Welfare League of Amer.*, Vol. l, No. 4, April.

ANDRY, R. G. (1962) 'Paternal & maternal roles & delinquency', in *Deprivation of Maternal Care*, Geneva: World Health Organisation.

ANTHONY, E. J. (1968) 'Group therapeutic techniques for residen- tial units', in *Disturbed Children*, ed. R. Tod.

ANTHONY, E. J. & KOUPERNIK, C. (eds) (1970) *The Child in his Family*, New York: Wiley-Interscience.

ANTROBUS, P. (1964) 'Coloured children in care', *Case Conference*, Vol. 11, No. 2, June.

ARGYLE, M. (1967) *The Psychology of Interpersonal Behaviour*, Penguin Books. (1969) *Social Interaction*, London: Methuen.

AXLINE, V. (1947) *Play Therapy: the inner dynamics of childhood*, Boston: Houghton Mifflin. (1966) *Dibs: in Search of Self*, London: Gollancz.

BALBERNIE, R. (1966) *Residential Work with Children*, Oxford: Pergamon.

BALL, G. & BAILEY, J. (1971) 'A group of experienced foster parents', in *Social Work in Foster Care*, ed. R. Tod.

BARNARDO'S (1966) *Racial Integration & Barnardo's*, Working party report, London: Barnardo's.

BARTLETT, H. (1970) *The Common Base of Social Work Practice*, New York: Nat. Assoc. Social Workers.

BEARD, R. M. (1969) *An Outline of Piaget's Developmental Psychology*, London: Routledge & Kegan Paul.

BEECH, H. R. (1969) *Changing Man's Behaviour*, Penguin Books.

BEEDELL, C. (1970) *Residential Life with Children*, London: Routledge & Kegan Paul.

BERNSTEIN, B. (1970) 'Elaborated & restricted codes: their social origins and some consequences', in *Readings in Child Socialization*, ed. K. Danziger.

BERNSTEIN, B. & YOUNG, D. (1967) 'Social class differences in conceptions of the uses of toys', *Sociology*, Vol. 1, No. 2, May.

BETTELHEIM, B. (1950) *Love is Not Enough*, London: Collier-Macmillan.

BOARD OF SOCIAL RESPONSIBILITY, *A Service of Blessing upon the Adoption of a Child*, London: Church Information Office.

BOND, N. A. (1969) 'A playgroup for fathers', *New Society*, 13 March.

BOSS, P. (1971) *Exploration into Child Care*, London: Routledge & Kegan Paul.

BOWLBY, J. (1946) *Forty-Four Juvenile Thieves, their Character & Homelife*, London: Baillière. (1951) *Maternal Care & Mental Health*, Geneva: WHO Monograph Series No. 2. (1965) *Child Care & the Growth of Love*, 2nd edition, Penguin

Books. (1958) 'Psycho-analysis & child care', in *Psycho-analysis and Contemporary Thought*, ed. J. Sutherland, London: Hogarth. (1960) 'Grief & mourning in infancy & early childhood', *Psycho-anal. Study Child*, Vol. 15, pp. 9-52. (1969) *Attachment & Loss, vol. 1: Attachment*, London: Hogarth/Penguin.

BRILL, K. & THOMAS, R. (1964) *Children in Homes*, London: Gollancz.

BURLINGHAM, D. & FREUD, A. (1944) *Infants without Families—the case for & against residential nurseries*, London: Allen & Unwin.

BURN, M. (1956) *Mr Lyward's Answer*, London: Hamish Hamilton.

BURNS, C. (1971) 'White staff, black children—is there a problem?' *J. Child Welfare League of Amer.*, Vol. l, No. 2, Feb.

BURTON, L. (1968) *Vulnerable Children*, London: Routledge & Kegan Paul.

CAPLAN, G. (1961) *An Approach to Community Mental Health*, London: Tavistock Publications.

CAPLAN, G. & LEBOVICI, S. (eds) (1969) *Adolescence: Psychosocial Perspectives*, New York: Basic Books.

CARLBACH, J. (1970) *Caring for Children in Trouble*, London: Routledge & Kegan Paul.

CARTER, W. (1971) 'Group counselling for adolescent foster children', in *Social Work in Foster Care*, ed. R. Tod.

CHARNLEY, J. (1955) *The Art of Child Placement*, Minneapolis: Univ. Minnesota Press.

CLEGG, A. & MEGSON, B. (1968) *Children in Distress*, Penguin Books.

COATES, K. & SILBURN, R. (1970) *Poverty: The Forgotten Englishmen*, Penguin Books.

COOPERSMITH, S. (1967) *The Antecedents of Self-Esteem*, San Francisco: Freeman.

COURT, J. (1969 a) 'Battering parents', *Social Work*, Vol. 26, No. 1, Jan. (1969 b) 'The battered child research project', *Child Care News*, No. 88, July.

COVENEY, P. (1967) *The Image of Childhood*, Penguin Books.

CRAFT, M., RAYNOR, J., COHEN, L. (eds) (1967) *Linking Home & School*, London: Longmans.

DANIEL, M. (1964) 'Casework with sick children & their parents', *Case Conference*, Vol. 10, No. 8, Feb.

DANZIGER, K. (ed.) (1970) *Readings in Child Socialization*, Oxford: Pergamon.

DAVIES, J. W. D. (1963) 'Reality & the deprived child', *Case Conference*, Vol. 10, No. 2, June. (1966) 'Group work & the deprived child', *Case Conference*, Vol. 12, No. 7, Jan. (1967) 'Thursday's child has far to go', *Case Conference*, Vol. 14, No. 8, Dec.

DAVIES, J. & JORGENSEN, J. (1970) 'Battered but not defeated', *J. Child Welfare League of Amer.*, Vol. xlix, No. 2, Feb.

DILLOW, L. (1971) 'The group process in adoptive homefinding', in *Social Work in Adoption*, ed. R. Tod.

DINNAGE, R. (1971) *The Handicapped Child: Research Review, Vol. 1, Neurological Handicaps*, London: Longmans.

DINNAGE, R. & PRINGLE, M. L. KELLMER (1967 a) *Foster Home Care—Facts & Fallacies*, London: Longmans. (1967 b) *Residential Child Care—Facts & Fallacies*, London: Longmans.

DOCKAR DRYSDALE, B. (1968) *Therapy in Child Care*, Papers on Residential Work Vol. 3, London: Longmans.

DOUGLAS, T. (1970) *A Decade of Small Group Theory, 1960-70*, London: Bookstall Publications.

DYER, E. (1965) 'Parenthood as crisis: a re-study', in *Crisis Intervention: Selected Readings*, ed. H. Parad.

ELLIS, J. (1971) 'Fostering of West African children', *Social Work Today*, Vol. 2, No. 5, 3 June.

ELLISON, M. (1958) *The Adopted Child*, London: Gollancz.

ERIKSON, E. H. (1950) *Childhood & Society*, Penguin Books. (1968) *Identity, Youth & Crisis*, London: Faber & Faber.

ESCALONA, S. K. (1969) *The Roots of Individuality*, London: Tavistock Publications.

ETZIONI, A. (1968) 'Basic human needs, alienation & inauthenticity', *Amer. Sociol. Review*, Vol. 33, No. 6, pp. 870-85, Dec.

EYSENCK, H. J. & RACHMAN, S. (1965) *The Causes & Cures of Neurosis*, London: Routledge & Kegan Paul.

FANSHEL, D. (1971) 'The exit of children from foster care—an interim research report', *J. Child Welfare League of Amer.*, Vol. l, No. 2, Feb.

FARBER, B. (1970) 'Marital integration as a factor in parent-child relations', in *Readings in Child Socialization*, ed. K. Danziger.

FERGUSON, T. (1966) *Children in Care—& After*, London: Oxford University Press.

FITZHERBERT, K. (1967) *West Indian Children in London*, Occas. Papers on Soc. Admin., No. 19, London: Bell.

FLINT, B. (1967) *The Child & the Institution*, University of London Press.

FONTANA, V. *et al.* (1963) 'The maltreatment syndrome in children', *New Eng. J. Med.*, Vol. 269, No. 26, pp. 1389-94, Dec.

FOREN, R. & BAILEY, R. (1968) *Authority in Social Casework*, Oxford: Pergamon.

FOREN, R. & BATTA, I. (1970) 'Colour as a variable in the use made of a local authority child care dept.', *Social Work*, Vol. 27, No. 3, July.

FRAIBERG, S. (1959) *The Magic Years*, London: Methuen.

FURNEAUX, B. (1969) *The Special Child*, Penguin Books.

GEORGE, V. (1970) *Foster Care: theory & practice*, London: Routledge & Kegan Paul.

GINOTT, H. (1965) *Between Parent & Child*, London: Pan Books.

GLICKMAN, E. (1957) *Child Placement through Clinically Oriented Casework*, New York: Columbia University Press.

GOFFMAN, E. (1963) *Stigma*, Penguin Books.

GOLDBERG, E. M. (1968) 'Working with the family in the child care field—concepts, methods & practice', *Social Work*, Vol. 25, No. 1, Jan.

GOODACRE, I. (1966) *Adoption Policy & Practice*, London: Allen & Unwin.

GREENWAY, E. (1966) 'Report on my work' (at High Wick Unit for severely disturbed children), *New Era*, Vol. 47, No. 1, Jan.

HALLIWELL, R. (1969) 'Time limited work with a family at the point of prosecution for neglect', *Case Conference*, Vol. 15, No. 9, Jan.

HALSEY, A. H. (1958) 'Genetics, social structure & intelligence', *Brit. J. Sociology*, Vol. 9, pp. 15-28.

HAZEL, N. (1968), 'Institutional care—for whose benefit?', *Case Conference*, Vol. 15, No. 3, July.

HEINICKE, C. & WESTHEIMER, I. (1965) *Brief Separations*, London: Longmans.

HELFER, R. (1970) 'A plan for protection—the child abuse center', *J. Child Welfare League of Amer.*, Vol. xlix, No. 9, Nov.

HELFER, R. & KEMPE, C. H. (eds) (1968) *The Battered Child*, University of Chicago Press. (1971) *Helping the Battered Child & his Family*, University of Chicago Press.

HENDERSON, J. & LEACH, A. (1971) 'The Thursday club—an experiment in social group work', *Social Work Today*, Vol. 1, No. 12, March.

HEWETT, S. & NEWSON, J. & E. (1970) *The Family & the Handicapped Child*, London: Allen & Unwin.

HEYWOOD, J. (1959) *Children in Care*, London: Routledge & Kegan Paul.

HILL, R. (1965) 'Generic features of families under stress', in *Crisis Intervention: Selected Readings*, ed. H. Parad.

HITCHMAN, J. (1960) *The King of the Barbareens*, Penguin Books.

H M S O (1969) *Youth & Community Work in the 70s.* (1970) *Adoption of Children*, working paper of Houghton Committee. (1970) *A Guide to Adoption Practice*, Advisory Council on Child Care, No. 2. (1970) *Care & Treatment in a Planned Environment*: a report on the Community Homes Project. (1971) *Fieldwork Training for Social Work: 6 discussion papers.*

HOLLIS, F. (1964) *Casework: A Psychosocial Therapy*, New York: Random House.

HOLMAN, R. (1964) 'Through a year with a child care officer', *Case Conference*, Vol. 11, No. 5, Oct. (1966) 'The child & the child care officer', *Case Conference*, Vol. 13, No. 2, June. (1968) 'Immigrants & child care policy', *Case Conference*, Vol. 15, No. 7, Nov. (1970) *Unsupported Mothers & the Care of their Children*, London: Mothers in Action.

HOLMAN, R. (ed.) & LAFITTE, F., SPENCER, K., WILSON, H. (1970) *Socially Deprived Families in Britain*, London: Bedford Square Press.

BIBLIOGRAPHY

HOLME, A. & MASSIE, P. (1970) *Children's Play—a study of needs & opportunities*, London: Michael Joseph.

HOLTOM, C. (1968) 'The participation of the natural family in the life of the child in care & in rehabilitation', *Child Care News*, No. 80, Nov.

HOPKIRK, M. (1949) *Nobody wanted Sam*, London: John Murray.

HOWARTH, E. *et al.* (1962) *The Canford Families: A Study in Social Casework & Group Work*, Sociological Review: Monograph No. 6: Univ. Keele.

HUGHES, A. (1967) 'The battered baby syndrome', *Case Conference*, Vol. 14, No. 8, Dec.

HUMPHREY, M. (1969) *The Hostage Seekers*, London: Longmans.

HUTCHINSON, P. (1969) 'The social worker & culture conflict', *Case Conference*, Vol. 15, No. 12, April.

INGRAM, E. (1961 a) 'Play & leisure time in the Children's Home', *Case Conference*, Vol. 7, No. 7, Jan.; also in *Children in Care*, ed. R. Tod. (1961 b) 'Living together in the Children's Home', *Case Conference*, Vol. 7, No. 8, Feb.

IRVINE, E. (1964) 'Children at risk', *Case Conference*, Vol. 10, No. 10, April; also in *Crisis Intervention: Selected Readings*, ed. H. Parad and in *Social Work with Families*, ed. E. Younghusband. (1967) 'The hard-to-like family', *Case Conference*, Vol. 14, No. 3, July.

ISAACS, S. (1933) *Social Development in Young Children*, London: Routledge & Kegan Paul. (1948) *Childhood & After*, London: Routledge & Kegan Paul.

JEANS, M. (1969) 'Grief & loss in families of subnormal children', *Case Conference*, Vol. 15, No. 10, Feb.

JEHU, D. (1963) *Casework before Admission to Care*, ACCO monograph No. 1, Assoc. Child Care Officers. (1967) *Learning Theory & Social Work*, London: Routledge & Kegan Paul. (1968) 'Childhood phobias—treatment in residential settings', *Child Care Qu. Review*, Vol. 22, No. 3, July.

JENKINS, R. (1963) 'The fostering of coloured children', *Case Conference*, Vol. 10, No. 5, Oct. (1965) 'The needs of foster parents', *Case Conference*, Vol. 11, No. 7, Jan. (1969) 'Long term fostering', *Case Conference*, Vol. 15, No. 9, Jan.

JENKINS, S. (1969) 'Separation experiences of parents whose children are in foster care', *J. Child Welfare League of Amer.*, Vol. xlviii, No. 6, June.

JOHNSON, B. (ed.) (1968) *The Evacuees*, London: Gollancz.

JONES, A. (1970) *School Counselling in Practice*, London: Ward Lock.

KADUSHIN, A. (1967) *Child Welfare Services*, New York: Macmillan. (1970) *Adopting Older Children*, New York: Columbia University Press.

KAHN, J. & NURSTEN, J. (1968) *Unwillingly to School*, Oxford: Pergamon.

KAY, N. (1966) 'A systematic approach to selecting foster parents', *Case Conference*, Vol. 13, No. 2, June; also in *Social Work in Foster Care*, ed. R. Tod. (1967) 'Foster parents as resources', *Case Conference*, Vol. 14, No. 6, Oct.; also in *Social Work in Foster Care*, ed. R. Tod. (1969) 'Behaviour therapy—another viewpoint', *Child Care News*, No. 89, Aug. (1970) 'The impact of compulsory removal of children on family cohesion', *Social Work*, Vol. 27, No. 1, Jan.

KEITH-LUCAS, A. (1961) 'More, not less, emphasis on parents' rights', *J. Child Welfare League of Amer.*, Vol. xl, Sept.

KEMP, C. (1971) 'Family treatment within the milieu of a residential treatment center', *J. Child Welfare League of Amer.*, Vol. l, No. 4, April.

KEMPE, C. H. *et al.* (1962), 'The battered child syndrome', *J. Am. Med. Assoc.*, Vol. 181, No. 1, pp. 17-24, July.

KERSHAW, J. (1961) *Handicapped Children*, London: Heinemann.

KIRK, H. D. (1964) *Shared Fate*, London: Collier-Macmillan.

KITZINGER, S. (1969) 'Communicating with immigrant mothers', in *Caring for Children*, ed. M. L. K. Pringle.

KLEIN, D. & ROSS, A. (1965) 'Kindergarten entry: a study of role transition', in *Crisis Intervention: Selected Readings*, ed. H. Parad.

KLEIN, J. (1965) *Samples from English Cultures, Vol. 2, Child Rearing Practices*, London: Routledge & Kegan Paul.

KOHN, M. L. (1959) 'Social class & the exercise of parental authority', *Am. Sociol. Rev.*, Vol. 24, pp. 352-66.

BIBLIOGRAPHY

KONOPKA, G. (1968) 'Effective communication with adolescents in institutions', in *Children in Care*, ed. R. Tod.

LAING, R. D. (1961) *The Self & Others*, London: Tavistock Publications. (1969) 'How best to intervene?', *New Society*, 11 Sept.

LAVAN, A. (1970) 'Simultaneous groups in a child guidance clinic', *Social Work Today*, Vol. 1, No. 7, Oct.

LAWDER, E. (1970) 'Post-adoption counselling: a professional obligation', *J. Child Welfare League of Amer.*, Vol. xlix, No. 8, Oct.

LAYCOCK, A. L. (1970) *Adolescence & Social Work*, London: Routledge & Kegan Paul.

LAZARUS, R. (1966) *Psychological Stress & the Coping Process*, New York: McGraw-Hill.

LEE, LAURIE (1964) *The Firstborn*, London: Hogarth.

LEISSNER, A. (1967) *Family Advice Services*, London: Longmans.

LE MASTERS, E. (1965) 'Parenthood as crisis', in *Crisis Intervention: Selected Readings*, ed. H. Parad.

LENNARD, H., BEAULIEU, M. & EMBREY, N. (1970) 'Interaction in families with a schizophrenic child', in *Readings in Child Socialization*, ed. K. Danziger.

LINDEMANN, E. (1965) 'Symptomatology & management of acute grief', in *Crisis Intervention: Selected Readings*, ed. H. Parad.

LLOYD, K. (1965) 'Helping a child adapt to stress', in *Social Work with Families*, ed. E. Younghusband.

LOMAX-SIMPSON, J. (1964) 'Practical ways of fulfilling some of the needs of the child in care', *Case Conference*, Vol. 10, No. 7, Jan. (1966) 'Further ideas on ways of sharing one's life with the child in care', *Case Conference*, Vol. 12, No. 10, April.

LOWENBURG, M. (1968) 'Food means more than nutriture', in *Children in Care*, ed. R. Tod.

LYND, H. M. (1958) *On Shame & the Search for Identity*, London: Routledge & Kegan Paul.

MAAS, H. (1969) 'Children in long-term foster-care', *J. Child Welfare League of Amer.*, Vol. xlviii, No. 6, June.

MAAS, H. & ENGLER, R. (1959) *Children in Need of Parents*, New York: Columbia University Press.

MACLAY, D. T. (1970) *Treatment for Children*, London: Allen & Unwin.

MCCULLOUGH, M. & ELY, P. (1968) *Social Work with Groups*, London: Routledge & Kegan Paul.

MCMICHAEL, J. (1971) *Handicap: a study of physically handicapped children & their families*, London: Staples Press.

MCWHINNIE, A. (1967) *Adopted Children—how they grow up*, London: Routledge & Kegan Paul. (1969) 'The adopted child in adolescence', in *Adolescence: Psychosocial Perspectives*, ed. G. Caplan & S. Lebovici. (1971) 'Group counselling with 78 adoptive families', in *Social Work in Adoption*, ed. R. Tod; also in *Case Conference*, Vol. 14, Nos. 11 & 12, March & April.

MCWHINNIE, J. (1969) 'Forms of language usage in adolescence & their relation to disturbed behaviour & its treatment', in *Adolescence: Psychosocial Perspectives*, ed. G. Caplan & S. Lebovici.

MALEWSKA, H. & MUSZYŃSKI, H. (1970) 'Children's attitudes to theft', in *Readings in Child Socialization*, ed. K. Danziger.

MALONE, B. (1971) 'Help for the child in an in-between world', in *Social Work in Foster Care*, ed. R. Tod.

MAPSTONE, E. (1971) 'Social work with the parents of children in foster care', in *Social Work in Foster Care*, ed. R. Tod.

MARSDEN, D. (1969) *Mothers Alone*, Penguin Books.

MAYER, J. & TIMMS, N. (1970) *The Client Speaks*, London: Routledge & Kegan Paul.

MIDDLETON, N. (1971) *When Family Failed*, London: Gollancz.

MILLAR, S. (1968) *The Psychology of Play*, Penguin Books.

MILLER, D. (1964) *Growth to Freedom: the psychosocial treatment of delinquent youth*, London: Tavistock Publications.

MILLOY, M. (1971) 'A look at the family & family interviewing', *J. Child Welfare League of Amer.*, Vol. l, No. 1, Jan.

MORRISH, I. (1971) *The Background of Immigrant Children*, London: Allen & Unwin.

MORRISSEY, J. (1965) 'Death anxiety in children with a fatal illness', in *Crisis Intervention: Selected Readings*, ed. H. Parad.

MULLER, P. (1969) *The Tasks of Childhood*, London: Weidenfeld & Nicolson.

MUSGROVE, F. (1964) *Youth & the Social Order*, London: Routledge & Kegan Paul.

MUSSEN, P. (1963) *The Psychological Development of the Child*, New Jersey: Prentice-Hall.

NEEL, A. (1971) 'Trends & dilemmas in child welfare research', *J. Child Welfare League of Amer.*, Vol. 1, No. 1, Jan.

NEWSON, J. & E. (1963) *Patterns of Care in an Urban Community*, London: Allen & Unwin/Penguin. (1968) *Four Years Old in an Urban Community*, London: Allen & Unwin.

NURSTEN, J. (1964) 'Role conflict in adolescence', *Social Work*, Vol. 21, No. 4, Oct.

OLSHANSKY, S. (1965) 'Chronic sorrow: a response to having a mentally defective child', in *Social Work with Families*, ed. E. Younghusband.

OPIE, I. & P. (1959) *The Lore & Language of Schoolchildren*, Oxford: Clarendon Press. (1969) *Children's Games in Street & Playground*, Oxford: Clarendon Press.

PACKMAN, J. (1968) *Child Care: Needs & Numbers*, London: Allen & Unwin.

PARAD, H. (ed.) (1965) *Crisis Intervention: Selected Readings*, New York: Family Service Assoc. of America.

PARFIT, J. (1971) *Spotlight on Physical & Mental Assessment*, Vol. 1, London: Nat. Children's Bureau.

PARKER, R. (1966) *Decision in Child Care*, London: Allen & Unwin. (1967) 'The residential care of children', *Case Conference*, Vol. 13, No. 9, Jan.

PARSONS, F. (1961) 'Residential child care: married staff and their children', *Case Conference*, Vol. 8, No. 5, Oct.

PERLMAN, H. H. (1966) 'Identity problems, role & casework treatment', in *New Developments in Casework*, ed. E. Younghusband. (1968) *Persona: Social Role & Personality*, University of Chicago Press.

PHILP, A. F. (1963) *Family Failure*, London: Faber & Faber.

PIAGET, J. (1959) *The Language & Thought of the Child*, 3rd edition, London: Routledge & Kegan Paul.

PICARDIE, M. (1969) 'Learning, communication & games', *Case Conference*, Vol. 15, No. 11, March.

PINCHBECK, I. & HEWITT, M. (1969) *Children in English Society*, Vol. I, London: Routledge & Kegan Paul.

PLANT, R. (1970) *Social & Moral Theory in Casework*, London: Routledge & Kegan Paul.

POCHIN, J. (1969) *Without a Wedding Ring*, London: Constable.

POLLACK, D. (1971) 'A sensitivity-training approach to group therapy with children', *J. Child Welfare League of Amer.*, Vol. l, No. 2, Feb.

PRESTAGE, R. O. (1964) 'Life for Kim', *Case Conference*, Vol. 10, No. 10, April.

PRINGLE, M. L. KELLMER (ed.) (1965) *Deprivation & Education*, London: Longmans. *Et al.* (1967) *Adoption: Facts & Fallacies*, London: Longmans. (ed.) (1969) *Caring for Children*, London: Longmans. (1970) 'Policy implications of child development studies', *Child Care News*, No. 94, Jan.

PRINGLE, M. L. K. & FIDDES, D. O. (1970) *The Challenge of Thalidomide*, London: Longmans.

PUGH (MAPSTONE), E. (1968) *Social Work in Child Care*, London: Routledge & Kegan Paul.

RABINOWITZ, A. (1969) 'Co-operation in a multi-purpose school for children aged 2-11 years with various handicaps', in *Caring for Children*, ed. M. L. K. Pringle.

RAYNOR, L. (1970) *Adoption of Non-White Children*, London: Allen & Unwin.

R C C A REVIEW (1962) *An ABC of Behaviour Problems*, Vol. 10: Resid. Child Care Assoc. (1967) *Play in Child Care*, Vol. 15: Resid. Child Care Assoc.

REID, W. J. & SHYNE, A. W. (1969) *Brief & Extended Casework*, New York: Columbia University Press.

REX, J. & MOORE, R. (1967) *Race, Community & Conflict*, London: Oxford University Press.

RICH, J. (1968) *Interviewing Children & Adolescents*, London: Macmillan.

RICHARDSON, E. (1967) *Group Study for Teachers*, London: Routledge & Kegan Paul.

ROBERTSON, J. (1958) *Young Children in Hospital*, London: Tavistock Publications.

ROGERS, C. (1965) *Client-centered Therapy*, Boston: Houghton Mifflin.

ROSEMAN, R. & COOKE, J. (1964) 'Social group work with children in a family casework agency', *Social Work*, Vol. 21, No. 4, Oct.

ROWE, J. (1959) *Yours by Choice—a guide for adoptive parents*, London: Routledge & Kegan Paul. (1966) *Parents, Children & Adoption*, London: Routledge & Kegan Paul. (1971) 'The reality of the adoptive family', in *Social Work in Adoption*, ed. R. Tod.

ROWE, J. & KORNITZER, M. (1968) 'Some casework implications in the study of children reclaimed or returned before final adoption', Standing Conf. Socs. Reg. for Adoption.

RUDDOCK, R. (1969) *Roles & Relationships*, London: Routledge & Kegan Paul.

RUTTER, M. (1966) *Children of Sick Parents*, London: Oxford University Press.

SALZBERGER-WITTENBURG, I. (1970) *Psycho-analytic Insight & Relationships*, London: Routledge & Kegan Paul.

SANDGRUND, G. (1971) 'Group counselling with adoptive families after legal adoption', in *Social Work in Adoption*, ed. R. Tod.

SANTS, H. (1964) 'Genealogical bewilderment in children with substitute parents', *Br. J. med. Psychol.*, Vol. 37, pp. 133-41.

SATIR, V. (1967) *Conjoint Family Therapy*, California: Science & Behaviour Books.

SCHAFFER, H. & E. (1968) *Child Care & the Family*, Occas. Papers on Soc. Admin. No. 25, London: Bell.

SCHEFF, T. (1966) *Being Mentally Ill*, London: Weidenfeld & Nicolson.

SCHNEIDER, E. (1969) 'Conjoint family therapy', *Case Conference*, Vol. 16, No. 6, Oct.

SCHREIBER, L. (1971) 'The H.E.L.P. line for parents', *J. Child Welfare League of Amer.*, Vol. l, No. 3, March.

SEARS, R., MACCOBY, E. & LEVIN, H. (1957) *Patterns of Child Rearing*, New York: Harper & Row.

SHAPIRO, P. (1963) 'Children's play as a concern of family caseworkers', *Case Conference*, Vol. 9, No. 7, Jan.; also in *Social Work with Families*, ed. E. Younghusband. (1968) 'Some illegitimate coloured children in long-term care', *Case Conference*, Vol. 15, No. 1, May.

SHARRAR, M. L. (1970) 'Some helpful techniques when placing older children for adoption', *J. Child Welfare League of Amer.*, Vol. xlix, No. 8, Oct.

SKINNER, A. & CASTLE, R. (1969) *78 Battered Children: A Retrospective Study*, London: NSPCC.

SKYNNER, A. C. R. (1971) 'Indications for & against conjoint family therapy'; 'A group analytic approach to conjoint family therapy'; 'The minimum sufficient network', *Social Work Today*, Vol. 2, Nos. 7, 8, 9, July.

SMITH, J. (1970 a) 'Short-term foster care as community work', *Case Conference*, Vol. 16, No. 9, Jan. (1970 b) 'Casework or reform', *Social Work Today*, Vol. 1, No. 3, June.

STANLEY, R. (1971) 'The group method in foster home studies', in *Social Work in Foster Care*, ed. R. Tod.

STEVENSON, O. (1963) 'The understanding caseworker', *New Society*, 1 Aug. (1965) *Someone Else's Child*, London: Routledge & Kegan Paul. (1968) 'Reception into care—its meaning for all concerned', in *Children in Care*, ed. R. Tod; also in *Case Conference*, Vol. 10, No. 4, Sept. 1963. (1971) 'Care or control: a view of intermediate treatment', *Social Work Today*, Vol. 2, No. 4, 20 May.

TALBOT, M. (1957) 'Panic in school phobia', *Amer. J. Orthopsychiat.*, Vol. 27, pp. 286-95.

THOMAS, C. (1971) 'Helping foster parents understand disturbed children', *J. Child Welfare League of Amer.*, Vol. l, No. 3, March.

THRASHER, F. (1963) *A Study of 1,313 Gangs in Chicago*, University of Chicago Press.

TILBURY, D. (1971) 'Selection of method in social work', *Social Work Today*, Vol. 2, No. 2, 22 April.

TIMMS, N. (1962) *Casework in the Child Care Service* (2nd edition 1969), London: Butterworth. (1964) *Social Casework: Principles & Practice*, London: Routledge & Kegan Paul.

TIZARD, J. & GRAD, J. (1961) *The Mentally Handicapped & their Families*, London: Oxford University Press.

TOD, R. (ed.) (1968 a) *Children in Care*—papers on residential work, Vol. 1, London: Longmans. (ed.) (1968 b) *Disturbed*

Children—papers on residential work, Vol. 2, London: Longmans. (ed.) (1971 a) *Social Work in Adoption* (collected papers) London: Longmans. (ed.) (1971 b) *Social Work in Foster Care* (collected papers) London: Longmans.

TRASLER, G. (1960) *In Place of Parents*, London: Routledge & Kegan Paul.

TRISELIOTIS, J. (1963) 'Immigrant schoolchildren & their problem of adjustment', *Case Conference*, Vol. 9, No. 7, Jan. (1970) *Evaluation of Adoption Policy & Practice*, University of Edinburgh.

TYNDALE, A. & PORTER, A. (1971) 'Group work with families who share a common problem', *Social Work Today*, Vol. 2, No. 2, 22 April.

ULLMANN, L. & KRASNER, L. (eds) (1965) *Case Studies in Behaviour Modification*, New York: Holt, Rinehart & Winston.

VANN, J. (1971) 'The child as a client of the social services dept.', *Br. J. Social Work*, Vol. 1, No. 2, Summer.

WALKER, A. (1967) 'Casework in residential schools for disturbed children', *Case Conference*, Vol. 13, No. 12, April. (1968) 'Social influences on disturbed immigrant children', *Case Conference*, Vol. 15, No. 6, Oct.

WALKER, L. (1970) *Bradford F S U Mothers' Group: group work with the inarticulate*, London: Family Service Units Paper No. 1.

WATSON, K. & BOVERMAN, H. (1971) 'Pre-adolescent foster-children in group discussions', in *Social Work in Foster Care*, ed. R. Tod.

WEINSTEIN, E. A. (1960) *The Self-Image of the Foster Child*, London: Russell Sage Foundation.

WESTHEIMER, I. (1970) 'Changes in response of mother to child during periods of separation', *Social Work*, Vol. 27, No. 1, Jan.

WIMPERIS, V. (1960) *The Unmarried Mother & her Child*, London: Allen & Unwin.

WINNICOTT, C. (1964) 'Casework techniques in the child care service', pp. 7-27; 'Casework & the residential treatment of children', pp. 28-39; 'Face to face with children', pp. 40-58, *Child Care & Social Work* (collected papers), London: Codicote/reprinted 1970, Bookstall Publications. (1968) 'Communicating with children', in *Disturbed children*, ed. R. Tod.

WINNICOTT, D. W. (1957) 'Two adopted children', *The Child & the Outside World*, London: Tavistock Publications. (1957/64) *The Child, the Family & the Outside World*, Penguin Books. (1971) *Playing & Reality*, London: Tavistock Publications.

WOLFF, S. (1969) *Children under Stress*, Penguin Books.

WOODMANSEY, A. C. (1966 a) 'The internalization of external conflict', *Int. J. Psycho-anal.*, Vol. 47, pp. 349-55. (1966 b) 'The transmission of problems from parents to children', in *Mental Illness in the Family: its Effect on the Child* (Proceedings of 22nd Child Guidance Inter-clinic Conference), London: Nat. Assoc. Mental Health. (1969) 'The common factor in problems of adolescence', *Br. J. med. Psychol.*, Vol. 42, pp. 353-70. (1971) 'Understanding delinquency', *Br. J. Criminology*, Vol. 11, No. 2, April.

WOOTTON, B. (1962) 'A social scientist's approach to maternal deprivation', in *Deprivation of Maternal Care*, Geneva: World Health Organisation.

WYNN, M. (1964) *Fatherless Families*, London: Michael Joseph. (1970) *Family Policy*, London: Michael Joseph.

YARROW, M., CAMPBELL, J. & BURTON, R. (1968) *Child Rearing—an enquiry into research & methods*, San Francisco: Jossey-Bass.

YOUNG, L. (1954) *Out of Wedlock*, New York: McGraw-Hill. (1964) *Wednesday's Children: a study of child neglect & abuse*, New York: McGraw-Hill.

YOUNGHUSBAND, E. (ed.) (1965) *Social Work with Families*, Readings in Social Work, Vol. 1, London: Allen & Unwin. (ed.) (1966) *New Developments in Casework*, Readings in Social Work, Vol. 2, London: Allen & Unwin.

YOUNGHUSBAND, E., BIRCHALL, D., DAVIE, R. & PRINGLE, M. L. K. (eds) (1970) *Living with Handicap*, London: National Children's Bureau.

BIBLIOGRAPHY

YUDKIN, S. (1967) *0-5: A Report on the Care of Pre-school Children*, London: Nat. Soc. Children's Nurseries, distributed by Allen & Unwin.